Discovering
The Dorset Coast

John Bailey

ACKNOWLEDGEMENTS

First and foremost I would like to acknowledge the generous and very kind offer to write the Foreword for the book from Brian Jackman, an award-winning journalist and author with a lifelong passion for travel and wildlife. Living in Dorset, Brian continues to write for *The Sunday Times*, but his work also appears in *The Daily Telegraph* and *BBC Wildlife Magazine*. Brian is also a Fellow of the Royal Geographical Society, a member of The British Guild of Travel Writers, a trustee of the George Adamson Wildlife Preservation Trust and a patron of Tusk Trust.

I would also like to show my appreciation to Martin Clunes for his kind words on *Discovering The Dorset Coast*.

I have met with and have received a tremendous amount of information and help from many characters along the journey and I would like to extend my gratitude to each and every one that has contributed in one form or another to the book.

For permission to include photographs of the interior of the old church at Fleet and Holy Trinity Church, and details of the flood, I would like to acknowledge the churchwardens and PCC of Holy Trinity, Fleet. I was as pleased as punch to include details of Professor Mark Poulton's famous Punch & Judy show at Weymouth and thank Mark for his help and contribution. The vast swathe of land from White Nothe in the west to Arish Mell in the east is privately owned by the Lulworth Estate, and I would like to mention my appreciation for their express permission for the use of photographs within the book of what is undoubtedly one of the most absorbing areas of the Dorset coast. None of these images should be reproduced without the express written permission of the Lulworth Estate.

For permission to include the photographs and the walk at Tyneham I would like to thank Richard Brooks, Senior Environmental Advisor at the Land Warfare Centre, and of course a thought must go out to the villagers who never returned to their homes. The Square and Compass, at Worth Matravers is home to a unique collection of Fossils and local finds and I would like to acknowledge the help and time from Kevin Hunt and Charlie Newman for access to information from the book *The Square and Compass, A Newman Century* available at the pub. The National Coastwatch Institution was set up in 1994 to restore a visual watch along the coast after many small coastguard stations were forced to close. I would like to acknowledge the information given by the volunteers at St Alban's Head and in particular to Mark & David at Peveril Point.

My thanks are extended to Andrew P.M. Wright, press officer and official photographer at the delightful Swanage Railway for his generous help and time, not only for checking the text for accuracy, but most of all for the permission to include the wonderful photographs of the locomotives looking their best in steam. The © copyright of those images remains with Andrew P.M. Wright and the Swanage Railway. I would like to thank Neil McCheyne at the Bournemouth-Swanage Motor Road and Ferry Company for detailed information on what is a most valuable service for both residents and visitors, providing a vital link between the Isle of Purbeck and Sandbanks. I would also like to mention Ali Tuckey, Ranger at Durlston Country Park, for his time and undoubted wealth of knowledge and enthusiasm, not only of the park and castle, but also of Swanage in general. I would also like to thank the kind assistance from Rachel Hardy at Bournemouth Tourism, www.bournemouth.co.uk

As in previous publication my appreciation once again is extended to Tina, my co photographer, and Nick for his help, to Julie Pack for her invaluable contribution of proof reading, and last but not least to Steve Caron and all the team at DB publishing.

Pages 74 & 77 *Photographs included with kind permission from the churchwardens and PCC of Holy Trinity Fleet.*
Page 88 *Image and text © copyright Mark Poulton and included with his kind permission.*
Page 89 *Images and text © copyright Mark Anderson and Sandworld and included with his kind permission.*
Pages 144–45 *Photographs included with kind permission of Charlie Newman, Square & Compass, Worth Matravers.*
Pages 152 *Photograph included with kind permission of Swanage RNLI Lifeboat Station.*
Pages 156–57 *Photographs included with kind permission of Durlston. www.durlston.co.uk*
Pages 158–59 *Photographs included with kind permission of Mary Buck, Swanage Cottage Hospital.*
Pages 160–67 *Photographs © Swanage Railway – Andrew P.M. Wright, and are included with his kind permission.*
Pages 178–81 *Text © The Bournemouth-Swanage Motor Road and Ferry Company, included with their kind permission.*

All mapping is included with permission from Ordnance Survey data © Crown copyright and database right 2012.

First published in Great Britain in 2012 by The Derby Books Publishing Company Limited, 3 The Parker Centre, Derby, DE21 4SZ.

ISBN 978-1-78091-013-0   Printed and bound by OzGraf, Poland.

Discovering
The Dorset Coast

John Bailey

Photography by John and Tina Bailey

Foreword by Brian Jackman

DB PUBLISHING

CONTENTS

FOREWORD

DORSET'S share of the South-West Peninsula Coast Path may be the shortest, but the 116km between Poole Harbour and the Devon border will take you on a roller-coaster journey past some of the richest, most varied and unusual coastal scenery to be found anywhere in Britain. No wonder the entire stretch from Devon to Old Harry Rocks became Britain's first and only natural World Heritage Site in 2001 – the Jurassic Coast – placing it in the same league as the Grand Canyon and the Great Barrier Reef.

My first view of Dorset's Heritage Coast was not from the land but from the rolling deck of an aircraft carrier half a century ago. As we rounded the limestone snout of Portland Bill, there rose the green hills behind Abbotsbury and the Chesil Beach, arching their backs like frightened cats, and the sheer cliffs beyond Burton Bradstock glowing yellow in the summer evening sunlight.

A decade or so later I came to live within a few miles of those same sandstone cliffs, having fallen headlong for this most beautiful of all Southern English counties. At that time I had only explored the coast in a somewhat desultory fashion, a few forays here and there and a bit of beachcombing around West Bay. But in the late 1970s I was commissioned by the Countryside Commission to write a guide to the Dorset Coast Path, and set out to walk it from end to end in easy stages. The result for me was a voyage of discovery that put the entire coast in perspective in a way that random day trips to the seaside can never do.

Compared to the long-distance paths of upland Britain the idea of a saunter along the Dorset coast sounded to me like a walk in the park; but how wrong I was. There are long stretches – on either side of Golden Cap and again between White Nothe and St Aldhelm's Head – where the cliffs roll like waves, the path plunging and soaring from sea level to cliff headland in a succession of heart-pumping ascents more suited to the Pennine Way. But there is no better way of getting to know the Dorset coast and exploring it is easy. Simply follow the signposts with the acorn symbol and don't go too close to the notoriously unstable cliff edges.

Start if you will at Lyme Regis, where Meryl Streep stood at the end of the Cobb, Lyme's crooked harbour wall, in *The French Lieutenant's Woman*, and where young Mary Anning, a Victorian fossil hunter dressed in bonnet and long dress unearthed the first ichthyosaurus known to science beneath the cliffs of Black Venn.

These Mesozoic sea monsters lived 200 million years ago when this was indeed Britain's Jurassic Park, its skies ruled by nightmarish pterosaurs with long, toothed beaks and leather wings. Now the day of the flying lizards is done, and their bones are entombed in the same rich fossil beds as those in which Mary Anning dug out ammonite shells the size of car tyres and bullet-shaped belemnites known in Victorian times as devil's fingers.

To the east, presiding over a chaos of landslips soars the leonine profile of Golden Cap, at 191m the highest cliff on the Channel coast. On a fine day when the gulls are wailing and the sea is an intense hyacinth blue there is no better spot for a breath of sea air, and the views are stupendous. On a clear day you can make out the rocks of Haytor on the roof of Dartmoor, and to the east the majestic sweep of Lyme Bay unfolds, with the waves breaking along the Chesil Beach, one of the geological wonders of Europe, a mighty ridge of tawny shingle running in an unbroken curve from West Bay to Portland.

But it is on the other side of Portland, between the golden sands of Weymouth Bay and the sheltered waters of Poole Harbour that the Dorset coast undergoes its most dramatic change. It starts at White Nothe above Ringstead Bay, where the chalk cliffs rise sheer from the sea, leading you on by way of Bats Head to the giant rock arch of Durdle Door and the equally famous Lulworth Cove.

Then comes what is arguably the grandest stretch of all – the high drama of the Purbeck coast between Gad Cliff and Anvil Point. Here, all is solid Jurassic limestone, carved into gaunt headlands, shadowy caverns and the sea-washed terraces of Dancing Ledge.

To this glorious mixture of ever-changing scenery add an equally varied handful of seaside resorts, from Lyme Regis at one end of the county to Bournemouth at the other, with Weymouth in between.

It was in Weymouth in 1789 that Mad King George III took his first royal swim in the sea, and although he didn't know it, as he emerged from the waves while a band played *God Save the King*, he had set a trend that would turn sea bathing into a national pastime and put Dorset on the map as the county where seaside holidays were invented.

Brian Jackman

INTRODUCTION

My first recollection of the sea comes from a visit to Dorset, the first of many that would follow during the early 1960s. A time I recall when the roads were quiet, and a journey of 70 miles was seen as an adventure, nowadays for some a mere commuting distance. Those early excursions instilled a deep affection for one of the most pastoral counties in England, and in particular the delightful seaboard, so it is with great affection that I return, to rediscover the beautiful Dorset coast.

Extending for over 80 miles from Lyme Regis in the west to Bournemouth in the east the beautiful Dorset coastline is unparalleled anywhere in Britain for its vast diversification, dotted with small quintessential villages and larger traditional seaside resorts, while inland are a myriad of ancient monuments, and historic relics. Foremost rural with a scattering of villages, Dorset also caters for the traditional seaside holidaymaker with the town of Weymouth, situated as it is, boasting the finest small boat sailing waters in northern Europe. Weymouth along with its neighbour Portland was selected to host the 2012 Olympic and Paralympics Sailing competitions. Close to the Hampshire border in the east the larger conurbation of Bournemouth is in complete contrast to the tiny coastal settlements of Fleet, Burton Bradstock, Seatown and Eype.

Offering an intimate view of the magnificent coast of Dorset, the book unfolds many delights en route. The journey begins at the famous Cobb, Lyme Regis, a town well documented for discoveries of Ichthyosaur and Plesiosaur skeletons by Mary Anning in the early part of the 19th century. Continuing east the highest point on the entire south coast is soon reached at Golden Cap, its trig point revealing a modest height of 626ft above sea level.

Tiny fishing villages are a delight and after passing the spectacular shingle spit of Chesil Beach we enter the principle setting of the novels of Thomas Hardy, the author who was born near Dorchester. Beyond the Isle of Portland and Weymouth the coast path reverts to secluded isolation and takes in the geological wonders of Durdle Door and Lulworth Cove. As we continue further east the book uncovers the story behind the now deserted village of Tyneham, its residents giving up their homes at the end of the war, destined never to return. The Isle of Purbeck reveals many wonders, including oil exploration around Kimmeridge Bay and the restored Swanage Light Railway, rekindling the halcyon days of steam. A walk from Studland skirts Poole Harbour, one of several which lay claim to the title of the worlds largest, or second largest natural harbour, before crossing by ferry to Sandbanks, home to many famous celebrities. The final leg of the journey concludes in the bustling seaside resort of Bournemouth.

LYME REGIS

Our journey begins at Lyme Regis, the most westerly town of Dorset, at the mouth of the River Lym. The river rises in the valley of Uplyme and Yawl, where heavy rain and a natural spring can combine to provide a torrent of water, the river providing sufficient energy to power a watermill along its lower reaches. The mill dating from 1340 has been restored to working order, producing flour for the mills bakery. The River Lym also called Lim runs along a series of terraces and feeds the mill via a leat. The *Domesday Book* of 1086 makes mention of a mill in Lyme with records showing that the area once boasted upwards of a dozen working mills.

The first written account of the town dates from AD 774 with the land bordering the River Lym belonging to the monks of Sherborne Abbey, gifted it is said from Cynewulf who was King of Wessex from 757 until his death in 786. Long before this, the area was inhabited by Iron Age man with evidence uncovered at Pilsden Pen, the second highest point of Dorset some 7 miles north-east of Lyme Regis.

The Romans made reference to 'Lym Super Mare'. The town takes its name from the Lym, Lym meaning torrent of water with Regis added in 1284 as a result of a Royal Charter granted by Edward I. The charter was confirmed by Queen Elizabeth I in 1591.

The 13th century would see the town prosper, developing into a major port. The Cobb was severely damaged by storms in 1328 and this appears to be the first mention of the harbour, originally built by oak piles driven into the seabed and boulders stacked between the timbers. The Cobb was of vast importance to the economy of the town and surrounding villages, with the sea defence enabling a ship building industry to flourish during the 18th and 19th century.

The Cobb has suffered severe storm damage on several occasions, being swept away in 1377, an event that witnessed the destruction of many boats and structural damage to several properties. During the late 1600s the southern wall was added but suffered at the hands of a storm during 1792. The present structure of Portland stone was completed during the early 19th century.

The Duke of Monmouth landed at Lyme Regis at the start of his rebellion in 1685 in his attempt to overthrow James II who had become King of England, King of Scotland and King of Ireland after the death of his brother, Charles II. The Duke of Monmouth was the illegitimate son of Charles II and claimed that he should be the true heir to the throne. Monmouth's forces were subsequently defeated at the battle of Sedgemoor in Somerset on 6 July 1685, and he was executed for treason on 15 July. The battle of Sedgemoor is often mentioned as being the last battle fought on British soil, although this fact has been disputed citing the Jacobite rebellion of 1745.

Golden Cap provides a most striking backdrop to the harbour at Lyme Regis. The harbour was first mentioned as early as the 14th century.

Opposite: The lamp posts in Lyme Regis are evidence of the town's association with fossils.

The Cobb has been referred to as a harbour wall rich in history. Jane Austen had stayed in Lyme Regis holidaying with her parents in the early 1800s and the town featured in her novels *Northanger Abbey* and more famously *Persuasion* featuring the Cobb where Louisa Musgrove fell. There is a delightful story that Alfred Tennyson visited the town and as he was being taken to the spot where Monmouth had landed, Lord Tennyson was quoted as saying 'Don't talk to me of the Duke of Monmouth, show me where Louisa Musgrove fell'. *Persuasion* was written between late summer 1815 and late summer 1816. Jane Austen never lived to see the publication of *Persuasion* as she died at the age of 42 in July 1817. Her brother Henry Austen oversaw the publication a year later and it has been said that it was he who gave the novel its title.

The Cobb also featured in the 1969 novel and subsequent film *The French Lieutenant's Woman* written by local author John Fowles who moved to Lyme Regis in 1968, where he remained until his death in 2005. The romantic novel was set in 19th-century England, about Charles, a biologist who's engaged to be married, but falls in love with outcast Sarah; the film portraying what would become an iconic image of the Cobb, with Meryl Streep stood looking forlornly out to sea.

By the late 18th century Lyme Regis had become a popular seaside resort among the middle classes, with increasing numbers arriving each year. Locals would supplement their income by selling 'curios' — ammonites — to the wealthy tourists. Fossil collecting was fast becoming the fashion of the day, at first a pastime but eventually being transformed into science as more was beginning to be understood about geology and biology. The fossils were being discovered in the Blue Lias cliffs around Lyme Bay. Alternate layers of limestone and shale were laid down as sediment on a shallow seabed during the Jurassic period between 210 and 195 million years ago. Due to the nature of their composition the cliffs were unstable particularly during periods of heavy winter rains drawing collectors to the area due to the number of landslides that would occur, often exposing many fossils on the cliffs and on the beach.

The town is renowned for its fossil discoveries and its most noted resident has to have been Mary Anning. Mary was born in Lyme Regis on the 21 May 1799. Her father, a cabinet maker, supplemented his income searching the cliffs for fossils to sell to the tourists. Mary would eventually join her father and they would set up a table together with her brother Joseph outside their home to sell their 'curios' making extra money for the family.

In Jane Austen's *Persuasion* Louisa Musgrove jumps off the steps, falls and is concussed.

After the death of her father in 1810, said to have been as a consequence of a fall on the cliffs, Mary continued her hunt for fossils. At the tender age of 12 in 1811, along with her brother, she dug up a 4ft Ichthyosaur skull, Mary finding the 17ft remainder of the skeleton a few months later. The family received £23 for the find with the fossilized remains being displayed by a well known collector in London. The skull of the specimen can still be seen today in the Natural History Museum, London. Other discoveries would yield more complete skeletons of Ichthyosaurs and Plesiosaurus. Mary remained in Lyme Regis where it was said she only left once for a short trip to London.

Mary died in 1847 from breast cancer having gained the respect of the scientific world, with her death recorded by the Geographical Society, still a men only organisation until 1902. Her life is commemorated by a stained-glass window in the local church of St Michael the Archangel. The town holds an annual Mary Anning Day and a Lyme Regis fossil festival.

During the Victorian age of railway building, attempts were made to connect Lyme Regis to the main London and South-Western Railway as early as 1845. Success it seemed had eventually come with an Act of Parliament passed in 1871, allowing The Lyme Regis Railway Company to begin track laying in 1874. Local enthusiasm for the venture was said to have been lukewarm at best and the plan came to a halt in 1876.

Under renewed local pressure in 1898 an attempt was made to force the LSWR to support the line, and under the Axminster and Lyme Regis Railway order of 1899, permission was given for a branch line from Axminster running for a distance of 6¾ miles into Lyme Regis. Work began on the 19 June 1900, but due to delays by bad weather and the topography the branch line was not fully completed until 1903.

The route from Axminster in East Devon took in the hamlet of Combpyne where there was an intermediate halt, through the village of Uplyme before traversing the Cannington Viaduct, the main engineering feature on the line. The track then crossed the border into Dorset ahead of reaching Lyme Regis.

During the 1950s with the increase in private motor car ownership, passenger traffic began to decline and although summer excursions did help to maintain the line, in winter the railway was sadly uneconomical. All freight traffic was withdrawn in 1964 with the infamous Beeching axe falling upon the line on 29 November 1965. Dr Richard Beeching had been brought in by the government to reduce the running costs of British Rail, and although he identified in his 'The Reshaping of British Railways' report that modernisation of trunk routes should take place, he also recommended wholesale closure of what was known as little used uneconomical branch lines and closure of local stations on the remaining routes.

The spot where Meryl Streep stood, looking forlornly out to sea, in the film adaptation of John Fowles' *The French Lieutenant's Woman*. **The view from the end of the Cobb is awe inspiring, taking in Charmouth, and Golden Cap, then continues eastward to West Bay and Chesil Beach.**

Pleasure craft and working boats all waiting for the tide to turn. The Dorset coast is affected by semi-diurnal tides, tides that occur in the main twice daily. The tide is the result of the gravitational forces of the moon and sun and tidal heights change with the phases of the moon. The tidal ranges are greater here at Lyme Bay compared to further east at Poole and Bournemouth.

In the late 1700s a Doctor Russell had declared that sea water had extraordinary curative powers, noting the sea water at Lyme Regis to be of very high quality. At this time Bath was the major spa centre for the west of England, its population boosted by wealthy gentry during the summer months. In a bid to attract visitors, baths were opened to allow bathing, and in addition bathing machines were introduced on the beach. These were drawn into the water by donkeys, allowing the visitor to take to the waters. A move was set in place to improve the architecture of the town that was still predominantly Tudor style with many owners rebuilding the front elevation of their houses, in an attempt to emulate the elegance of Bath.

Mapatia left high and dry.

By the late 18th century Lyme Regis had become a popular seaside resort.

Today the official guide states 'Lyme Regis boasts breathtaking scenery and a special mystique, making it a sparkling resort for all seasons. Its historic Cobb and harbour are iconic features, set against moody blue cliffs yielding fossilized evidence of life on earth millions of years ago'. The old town dating from the 14th century is home to several shops and art galleries and a museum, with the recently refurbished mill built around the River Lym or Lim now fully operational.

The sea is, of course, the main attraction for visitors with bathers well catered for, thanks to an award-winning environmental protection scheme, ensuring safe and clean waters around Lyme's beaches. The Cobb is a haven for anglers and numerous boat trips can be taken from the harbour with deep sea fishing available or just a quiet trip around the bay.

Lyme Regis is a hive of activity with leisurely boat trips available around the bay or more adventurous deep sea fishing excursions from the quayside with an option to hire your own colourful means to view the bay.

Opposite: The harbour provides safe anchorage for many fishing and pleasure craft, their vivid colours help to create a striking scene.

Lyme Regis seen from Charmouth, as a late summers day draws to a close.

Black Venn between Lyme Regis and Charmouth is the site of one of the largest coastal mudslides in Europe. Between 1958 and 1959 two huge mudslides occurred, spilling out across the beach. The remains of those mud slides can still be seen today at low tide, when the boulder arcs become exposed. However, these cliffs continue to move and in 2008 a large section of the land slipped onto the beach causing a diversion of the south-west coastal path inland.

CHARMOUTH

Charmouth, a picturesque Dorset seaside village, our next destination, lies a short distance north-east of Lyme Regis. Evidence exists of Neolithic and Bronze Age settlers but it was the Iron Age people who left their mark on the area with impressive hill forts that are still visible today at Pilsden Pen and Maiden Castle.

The name originates from Cerne, meaning stony river. The River Char is fed by many tributaries that rise within the beautiful Marshwood Vale before flowing into the sea. The village, a planned mediaeval community, dates from the 13th century. The buildings today vary in age; some smaller cottages date from the 17th and 18th century while some Regency styled properties complement the architecture.

Charmouth is said to have been one of Jane Austen's favourite haunts with the distinguished author quoted as saying 'Charmouth, with its high grounds and extensive sweeps of the country, and still more, its sweet retired bay, backed with dark cliffs, where fragments of low rock among the sands make it the happiest spot for watching the flow of the tide'.

The Charmouth Heritage Coast Centre can be located on the foreshore, set up in 1985 to encourage the safe collecting of Jurassic fossils from the local beaches. The centre, as well as having a shop, provides a varied programme of fossil events and activities which run all year round, including fossil hunting walks and ammonite slice polishing sessions. The centre also displays information on the geology and coastal wildlife of the area. Entry to the centre is free, but as a charity your donations would be most welcome. The old stone building that houses the centre was originally a cement works, opened in 1850 but the business failed and the building soon fell into disrepair.

A little inland and high above the village north-east of Charmouth is Stonebarrow Hill. The site of an old radar station, now owned by the National Trust, can be found by taking the minor road on your right as you leave the village heading in the direction of Chideock.

Charmouth beach is the ideal family beach with a mixture of sand and pebbles.

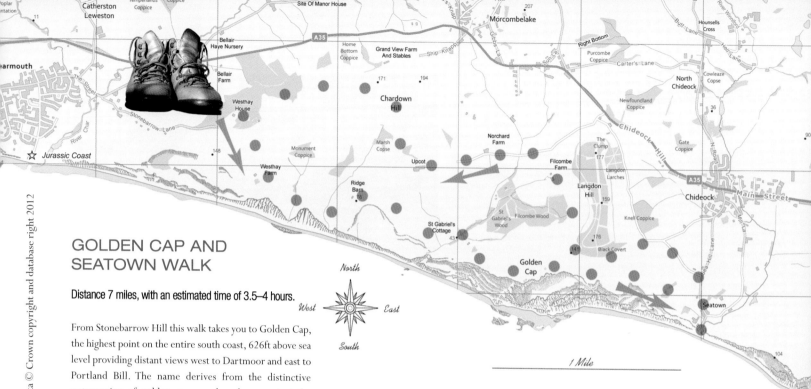

GOLDEN CAP AND
SEATOWN WALK

Distance 7 miles, with an estimated time of 3.5–4 hours.

From Stonebarrow Hill this walk takes you to Golden Cap, the highest point on the entire south coast, 626ft above sea level providing distant views west to Dartmoor and east to Portland Bill. The name derives from the distinctive outcropping of golden greensand rock present at the summit of the cliff face.

The route passes St Gabriel's Chapel before the somewhat demanding ascent begins with the reward for the effort clear to see in all directions. On descending from the summit your incentive is the tiny settlement at Seatown, where a rest can be taken at the Anchor Inn, originally a smugglers haunt, before continuing along quiet lanes that slip deep into Dorset valleys. Bordered by hedgerows on either side, their high grassy banks come alive in spring time with primrose and wood anemone, while the summer sun transforms them with swathes of foxgloves. The concluding part of the route is a steady climb to return to Stonebarrow Hill via Chardown Hill.

Park at the National Trust car park at Stonebarrow Hill (charges apply) where the trust has a shop and toilets at grid reference 383 934.

1 Mile

East from Charmouth the unstable cliffs of Stonebarrow and Golden Cap dominate the scene.

Charmouth hugs the hillside above Lyme Bay as you glance back over the first part of this exhilarating coastal amble.

Take the path heading towards the sea, signed coast path east, to descend past West Hay farm to reach the open expanse of Cain's Folly, where below can be seen the remains of the World War Two radar station, destroyed in the 1942 landslide. The coastal views on this section of the walk are magnificent. To the west Charmouth hugs the hillside and beyond Lyme Regis with the distinctive harbour walls and the distant cliffs of East Devon. Looking east the summit of Golden Cap and the distant Isle of Portland extends its rocky promontory far out into the English Channel.

Stanton St Gabriel was originally a Saxon settlement. The remnants of the chapel and a National Trust converted thatched cottage are all that remains today.

The route continues following the coastal path for a mile to reach St Gabriel's Mouth. St Gabriel's can be found by heading inland at this point. Stanton St Gabriel was originally a Saxon settlement, the remnants of the chapel and National Trust converted thatched cottages are all that remains today.

The tiny hamlet was recorded in the *Domesday Book* of 1086, with the first records of St Gabriel's Chapel dating from 1240. In the 16th century much reference can be found to repairs due to damage from storms, despite being built in a hollow. During the 17th century more than 20 families lived in the tiny hamlet relying on fishing and farming for their livelihoods but by the next century the population had left and the settlement fell into disrepair. It is believed that the end came for the hamlet when the coach road that passed this way between Bridport and Charmouth was replaced with a higher level new route passing through Morcombelake.

The National Trust renovated the cottages into holiday accommodation and restored a 19th-century sheep-wash close to the house.

Once you have soaked up the atmosphere of this tranquil hollow retrace your steps back to the coastal path to continue towards the summit of Golden Cap. The isolation of this stretch of coast would have been taken advantage of by the locals during the early 19th century. Where the Winniford stream runs to the sea meandering through the shingle, the men of Seatown and Chideock would have been fisherman by day, but by night, many were smugglers.

The contraband would be run ashore at St Gabriel's Mouth and transported up the valley between the tall cliffs of Golden Cap and Cain's Folly where it is said the ruined chapel was a favourite receiving house. The contraband would then be loaded on to pack horses, taken through the Marshwood Vale and further inland using the plethora of quiet bridleways and tracks.

The route now presents you with the toughest challenge, the ascent of Golden Cap, as you are only a little over 100ft above sea level at this point. Too late to mention now but from the car park at Langdon Hill the route to the summit of the south coast would be relatively easy. A path follows the contours around the hillside, where the fragrance of the blue-green pines on balmy summer days can allow your imagination to transport you to foreign climes, especially when set against the azure sea. Langdon Hill sits some 500ft above sea level. The wood was planted in the 1950s mainly of Corsican Pine on a site originally a copse, known locally as Elanor's Clump. The wood is now owned by the National Trust.

Below the summit of Golden cap is the tiny settlement at Seatown and beyond the undulating cliff tops of Dog House Hill and Thorncombe Beacon.

The walk to the summit does require some exertion from here but the views once atop are a generous return for your effort. A stone memorial on the summit bears the inscription 'Given by members of the National Trust and friends in memory of the Earl of Antrim KBE'. The Earl was chairman of the trust from 1966 until 1977. The trig point or triangulation pillar shows the height as 619ft above sea level, but is sat a little from the true summit. The views are spectacular and on a clear day East Devon and Dartmoor are visible, while the expansive golden shingle spit of Chesil Beach and Portland stand out bordered by the seeming limitless expanse of the English Channel. Seatown, just over a mile below, is the next destination and possible port of call and is soon reached, with the pace now increasing as you descend the cliff path. A minor diversion inland due to coastal erosion is noted as a temporary measure.

Trig points, or triangulation pillars, were built to assist an accurate geographical survey of Great Britain, beginning in 1935. The positioning of the trig point was such that at least two others could be seen from any one. By sitting a theodolite on the concealed mountings on top of the pillars, accurate bearing to the nearest trig points could be taken. This process called triangulation covered the whole country and led to the OS maps we use today. A benchmark was set on the side inscribed with the letters 'OSBM' (Ordnance Survey Bench Mark) and the reference number of the trig point.

This fine example of a windblown tree in a coastal location was here when I first visited Golden Cap in the 1970s. The route is well signposted as you head toward Seatown, now requiring a diversion due to erosion of the cliffs.

Seatown was once much larger than it is today, although never a town just a hamlet, situated less than a mile from the inland village of Chideock. All that remains today are a handful of cottages and the Anchor Inn, originally the haunt of smugglers and behind, strategically placed, was the Coastguard Station.

The sea has claimed many of the original buildings. An advance party from the Duke of Monmouth's fleet was said to have put ashore here in June 1685 ahead of docking at Lyme. Thomas Matthews from Chideock joined the doomed rebellion and was, as a consequence, imprisoned before being transported to Barbados.

The large anchor that has pride of place outside the inn was dredged up by a local fisherman who at the time had no inclination of the history attached, belonging as it did to the Dutch vessel *Hope*. The 350 tonne gun ship with a cargo of gold and silver was returning from Curacao to Amsterdam during the 18th century when it ran aground during a storm off Chesil Beach. The residents of the area would benefit from this disaster as we discover further east at Burton Bradstock.

The main attraction of Seatown today has to be its secluded beach sat at the foot of the valley, but the pebbled beach does shelve steeply, so care needs to be taken as there are no lifeguards. A swim on this stretch of the coast should not be underestimated and is not for the faint hearted. Even on calm days the undertow can be considerable, with many a swimmer being unceremoniously deposited onto the pebbled beach, while attempting to return to dry land.

The walk now follows Sea Hill Lane towards Chideock as it wends its way at first climbing steeply from this delightful setting. Continue up the hill bearing left onto Pettycrate Lane, the lane providing a haven for walkers with distant pastoral and sea views unfolding.

Golden Cap from Seatown, perhaps looking its most formidable when the seas are turbulent, and a glimmer of sun sets the hill against a heavily laden sky.

Seatown from the vantage point of Dog House Hill with the now distant town of Lyme Regis nestling amongst the cliffs across Lyme bay.

The winding lanes of Dorset are awash with wood anemone during spring, their leaves remaining well into summer. The plant takes its name from the Greek word for wind, anemos as the slender flowers shake in the wind.

The route passes a junction to Langdon Lane on your right and continues along Pettycrate Lane, by now merely a track skirting Langdon Wood, with its fragranced Corsican Pine a delight to the senses. At the end of the woods the path curves right to begin the descent of the hillside, heading all the while to the gap in the hedge, and then continues across another field. Pass through another gap to follow a track, with woodland now on your left. After Filcombe Farm the track continues, eventually emerging onto the delightful Muddeford Lane.

Follow this secret Dorset lane bedecked with wild flowers from spring to summer, for over half a mile ignoring the turning left that would take you down to St Gabriel's, to reach some farm buildings. Continue through the farm yard bearing right following the track uphill ignoring the first track on your left, the route wending its way up Chardown Hill to emerge at a car park.

Take the upper track that continues on a gentle incline back westward to arrive at the start point in a little under half a mile, with tremendous pastoral views of the Dorset countryside your constant companion.

The fragranced Corsican Pine of Langdon Wood are a delight to the senses.

MORCOMBELAKE

The journey along the Dorset coast continues eastward where the busy A35 meets the village of Morcombelake, nestled under Hardown Hill, with a delightful little chapel-like church within sight of the sea dating from 1841.

Morcombelake has two very different historical claims, the first being the square stone well known locally as St Wite's well. Local tradition has it that St Candida or Wite who gave her name to the nearby village of Whitchurch Canonicorum was a Saxon holy woman, who would have lived a reclusive life of prayer. She was reputedly killed by Danish raiders, who pillaged the area during the eighth century. The well has been said to provide healing powers with the waters particularly beneficial for sore eyes. The church of St Candida or St Wite in Whitchurch Canonicorum is unique, being the only parish church that retains the original mediaeval shrine and relics of its patron saint to whom it is dedicated.

Since the middle 1800s the Moores family have been baking biscuits in Dorset with a bakery established here in Morcombelake in 1880.

CHIDEOCK

The village of Chideock lies less than a mile inland from Seatown and is home to many substantial cob and sandstone cottages, some the perfect representation of the 'chocolate box' cottage with roses around the door. The *Domesday Book* mentions the settlement as Cidihoc with the name seeming changed several times over the last 900 years.

The area suffered a long history of religious strife during the English Civil War. The remains of what was once a Royalist castle are marked in a field to the north-east of the village off Ruins Lane. All that remains today are the earth mounds and a large cross erected in memory of the Chideock Martyrs. The second John De Chidiock built the castle in 1380, the lands having been given to the first John De Chidiock in 1312 from King Edward II. During the English Civil War the castle stood as a Royalist stronghold withstanding many attacks by the Parliamentarians until final capture in 1645. Legend has it that after the castle was destroyed by canon fire the locals used the stone to build their cottages.

Today the area caters well for the visitor. As we have already seen, Seatown has The Anchor Inn while within Chideock can be found The Clock House Inn, dating from the 16th century and The George Inn, a traditional Dorset thatched pub, popular with both locals and holidaymakers.

'Chocolate Box' cottages are a constant feature of Dorset's quintessential villages and none more so than here at Chideock.

These delightful cottages lead the way to the tiny coastal settlement of Seatown.

On leaving Seatown and Chideock, the road climbs east skirting the delightful market town of Bridport. A little over 2 miles from Chideock is the tiny village of Eype, as with Seatown, set delightfully off the beaten track, accessible only by narrow country lanes, or on foot if using the South West Coastal Path.

The origin of the name comes from 'Steep Place' and very little documented evidence exists about Eype, despite many properties in the village dating from the 18th century. To the west is Thorncombe Beacon, owned by the National Trust. The ancient beacon was one of a series positioned along the English Channel coast, part of an early warning system, in case of impending foreign invasion.

The beacon yields several species of ammonites to be found on the pebbled beach below the cliffs. Thorncombe Beacon stands a little over 500ft above sea level, a giant on the south coast but still some way short of its neighbour, Golden Cap.

Excavations have revealed on Doghouse Hill, between Seatown and Eype, that man lived here over 10,000 years ago, making it the oldest human settlement in West Dorset. A stone hearth and fire pit from the Bronze Age have been discovered, with other finds believed to date as far back as the Mesolithic Age. The Mesolithic peoples were hunter gatherers, at a time when the coastline here would have extended a further mile out to sea, however, due to coastal erosion over the last 8,000 years or so the site now lies perilously close to the cliff top, in danger of disappearing into the sea.

To the west of Eype is Thorncombe Beacon. The ancient beacon was one of a series positioned along the English Channel coast, part of an early warning system in case of impending foreign invasion.

This charming dwelling can be seen close to the bay.

BRIDPORT AND WEST BAY

The Middle Ages cover one of the most bloodthirsty periods of English history, beginning in 1066 with the battle of Hastings and the Norman Conquest and ends in the late 15th century, with the death of Richard III. It was during this eventful period that Bridport developed although a settlement existed on this site as early as the ninth century. The entry in the *Domesday Book* refers to Brideport with mention of Bredeport during the 13th century. Standing as it does at the confluence of the rivers Brit and Asker, the town was to become the country's most important rope making centre during the 13th century. Hemp and flax was grown locally with the importance of the towns industry highlighted in 1213 when King John urged the rope makers to work night and day to supply his navy.

Bridport rope was used for making the hangman's rope giving rise to the saying 'stabbed with a Bridport dagger'. During the reign of King Henry VIII an order went out that all cordage, ropes and the lines and rigging for his ships be made at Bridport or within 5 miles of it, and nowhere else. Net making was also a thriving industry helping to establish the town's fame and fortune.

The town received a royal charter granted by Henry II in 1253 and again in the 16th century, when a new charter from Queen Elizabeth I in 1554 confirmed the right for Bridport to hold a twice weekly market and three annual fairs, Old Lady Day, Holy Thursday and Old Michaelmas. The markets still survive, on Wednesdays and Saturdays.

The 18th century saw major development and rebuilding taking place with shipbuilding providing a boost to the local economy. The arrival of the railway in 1857 also added to the wealth of the town.

With the onslaught of cheaper foreign imports the hemp growing industry fell into decline as did the shipbuilding industry towards the end of the 19th century.

The parish church of St Mary is located in South Street. The records show that a church stood on this site during the Middle Ages, the earliest evidence dating from the 13th century.

The main structure, including the tower, dates from the prosperous 15th century. Within the Chapel is a brass plate commemorating Edward Coker who was killed in a skirmish by one of the Duke of Monmouth's officers in 1685. During the reign of Queen Victoria major restoration works were carried out on the church, although it was said that Thomas Hardy disapproved of the works.

Today the prosperous market town is a popular destination, with the visitors to the region well catered for. The town still continues to manufacture rope and nets, with local businesses supplying commercial fishing nets, construction safety net, and sports perimeter netting. The history of Bridport is well documented in the town museum.

A factoid is defined in the dictionary to be a small and often unimportant bit of information, perhaps a good example being that Bridport supplied the goal nets for England's World Cup victory in 1966. At the time it was definitely not unimportant, although maybe not needed for Geoff Hurst's second goal, they certainly were for his third and England's fourth.

The harbour is a busy place with a combination of working and pleasure craft.

CHARISMA
NEWHAVEN

WEST BAY
(BRIDPORT HARBOUR)

The first records of a harbour can be traced back to the 13th century with access along the River Brit, as Bridport was landlocked. During the 14th century a local merchant, John Huddersfield, began construction of a haven under instruction from King Richard II. During the 17th century the first piers were introduced with the area becoming known as Bridport Harbour.

In the mid 1700s plans were put forward for a permanent structure with the river diverted, sluices put in position and a ship building yard established. The 19th century saw an Act of Parliament allowing the purchase of land to build a larger harbour with construction completed in the early 1800s.

With the Bridport Railway Company extension to the harbour completed in 1884, and with ship building in decline, an attempt was made to transform the area into a holiday destination, with the GWR renaming the area as West Bay, a name that was already identified on some 19th-century Dorset maps.

The esplanade was built in 1887 with the new promenade constructed along the west cliff in 1967. In the 21st century the harbour has been strengthened with the new Jurassic pier completed in 2004, part of a multi-million pound coastal defence scheme offering stunning views east to Portland Bill and west as far as Brixham in Devon.

Working boats are much in evidence.

Lobster pots and crab pots on the quayside are evidence that West Bay is still a working port. The lobsters find their way in through a funnel to the main baited chamber, once in they are unable to find their way back out. The lobster pots are dropped onto the sea bed with floating buoys to enable their collection later.

West Bay was the location of the BBC television series called *Harbour Lights*, starring Nick Berry and the beach was used for the introduction of the original BBC television series, *The Fall and Rise of Reginald Perrin*.

A quintessential part of the charm
oozing from a rural Dorset railway
station would be the picket fence
adjoining the platform, almost certainly
entwined in wild roses.

In 1845 a plan was put forward to build a branch line linking Bridport to the main line at Maiden Newton, a distance of a little over 9 miles. The Bridport Railway Company was formed and the requisite Act of Parliament was passed on 5 May 1855. The company opted for the 7ft ¼in broad gauge and estimated an ambitious completion of the project by the autumn of 1856. Major earthworks had to be undertaken and the project was to be delayed by a year. Further issues had to be overcome resulting in an additional delay with the official opening taking place in November 1857. The Great Western Railway (GWR) supplied the traction and rolling stock.

The branch line had one station along the entire route at Powerstock with a second added at Toller Porcorum in 1862. Across Britain the standard gauge of 4ft 8½in was being introduced with a Royal Commission reporting in 1845 in favour of a standard gauge in Britain, electing George Stephenson's 4ft 8½in over the 7ft ¼in. One reason cited was that the current length of the entire rail system in Britain had eight times more track using the standard gauge. The track was modified to the standard gauge during the summer of 1874.

The success of the Bridport branch line prompted an extension to the coast, with the ultimate aim of promoting Bridport into a holiday destination. It was decided to name the new station built at Bridport harbour, West Bay, as by this time the harbour was in decline, taking the name from the bay at the eastern end of Chesil Beach close to Portland. The new station was opened in March 1884 with the local public house being renamed The West Bay Hotel.

By the end of the 19th century most of the small independent railway companies had been bought out, amalgamated into the larger companies, and by 1901 the company had become part of the GWR. The line survived until 1930 when the decision was taken to close the Bridport to West Bay section for passenger traffic, keeping it open only for goods traffic, 1962 saw the final closure with the track lifted in 1965.

The infamous Dr Beeching Report of 1963 recommended closure of the remaining section of the branch line, but due to the restricted road access in the area, it remained defiantly open becoming the last surviving branch line in Dorset. By 1975, however, the line had become totally uneconomical, closing ironically 120 years to the day of the original passing of the Act of Parliament that gave it life.

West Bay Station still exists today, renovated and operating as a tea station.

The last surviving branch line in Dorset eventually closed in 1975. Nonetheless the station and some of the infrastructure remains today, albeit serving as a tea room.

BURTON BRADSTOCK

Situated at the western extreme of Chesil Beach, nestled in the beautiful Bride Valley, we come upon the quintessential Dorset village of Burton Bradstock, with its picture postcard stone cottages and flower filled English country gardens. The original village is thought to date from Saxon times, then known as Brideton, derived from the village of the River Bride. The *Domesday Book* commissioned in 1085 by William the Conqueror, who had invaded England in 1066, and completed in 1086, recorded 13,148 settlements across England, including as it was known at the time, Bridetona. Bradstock originates from Bradenstoke Priory in Wiltshire, the association stemming from the time when land from the parish was passed to the Priory. The original part of the pretty village remains unspoilt with a cluster of thatched cottages dating from the 16th and 17th centuries, with the church of St Mary the Virgin at its heart. The greater part of St Mary's dates from the prosperous 15th century although some parts date back to the previous 14th century. With few exceptions the delightful mellow stone thatched cottages in the historic centre of the village were built using the local stone that dates from circa 180 million years, formed as sediments of clay, sand or mud under a shallow sea on a continental shelf.

The sea, as would be expected, has played a large part in the rich history of the village and legends of the activities of smugglers abound, with Burton Bradstock seen as a strategic landing place for contraband during the 18th and 19th century, situated as it is at the midpoint of Lyme Bay. Another profitable trade was from shipwrecks as the coastal waters off Chesil Beach are some of the most dangerous in Britain, particularly when storms move in from the south-west. The shingle spit as we will discover later runs for some 16 miles and has claimed upward of 200 wrecks, with stories of looting commonplace. One such event took place in 1749 when the Dutch vessel *Hope* encountered storms in the English Channel running aground onto Chesil Beach, carrying gold to the value of £50,000. The sailing ship broke apart, with the upper deck coming to rest on the ridge of pebbles, and the cabin buried in the sands. It was reported that the hull was never found, presumed swept back out to sea. Despite the catastrophe, all of the crew made it safely ashore. The word soon spread with estimates of as many as 10,000 people from all parts of the county, all searching for a share of the bounty descending on the area. After 10 days, Justices of the Peace, with a body of armed men dispersed the looters.

The original village is thought to date from Saxon times then known as Brideton, derived from the village of the River Bride.

Being at the centre of Hitler's planned invasion area, Burton Bradstock became host to many British, American and Canadian troops leading up to the D-Day landings, with our next destination Chesil Beach revealing its role in the outcome of the war. As throughout Britain, Burton Bradstock would witness the sad loss of a large number of villagers during World War Two, as it had done previously during the 1914–18 campaign. To mark the 50th anniversary of D-Day the seat around the tree on the village green was extended by the parish council to recall the US troops billeted in the village, and their training in the area.

The tree on the village green has a memorial seat, commemorating the accession of Edward VII in 1902.

Mellow evening sun envelopes the Post Office on Mill Street.

The cipher on the post box dates installation during the reign of King George V between the years 1910–36. George was the grandson of Queen Victoria, and on her death in 1901, George's father became King Edward III, and George was made Prince of Wales. On his father's death in 1910, he succeeded Edward as King.

The quintessential Dorset village of Burton Bradstock, with its picture postcard stone cottages and flower filled English country gardens.

Roses around the door are the archetypal vision of the English country cottage. No other flower is as rich in poetic and legendary significance as the rose. The rose represents romance, love, beauty and elegance, and has featured in myths, folklore and religion, for centuries having been the much cherished flower of poets and artists.

The cliffs at Burton Hive present a good example of the distinctive, alternate hard and soft layers of the Bridport Sand, which takes on the appearance of bright gold in sunlight.

This Dorset fingerpost has seen better days but still guides the visitor in the right direction. The roundel on top is a feature that becomes more prominent as we travel further east.

The shingle at the western extreme of Chesil Beach is pea size gaining in size as the shingle spit progresses eastwards.

47

HIVE BEACH
(BURTON BRADSTOCK)

The beach at the most westerly point of Chesil Beach is known as Hive Beach, the coast of the village of Burton Bradstock. The shingle beach is surrounded by spectacular sandstone cliffs. The cliffs present a good example of the distinctive alternate hard and soft layers of the Bridport Sand, which takes on the appearance of bright gold in sunlight.

Regular rock falls will often expose a new source of ammonites on the beach. The area around Hive Beach is popular with visitors, and has a local seafood restaurant now open all year, delightfully situated above the shingle beach. The beach does shelf steeply so care should be taken, if attempting to swim, due to the strong undercurrents. The cliffs provide the option for several miles of spectacular picturesque coastal walking, west to West Bay and Seatown, or alternatively east along the relatively flat expanse behind Chesil Beach, to West Bexington.

The beach here shelves steeply so care should be taken if attempting to swim due to the strong undercurrents.

The road to Abbotsbury provides several opportunities for stunning views along Chesil Beach but equally west to Thorncombe Beacon and the unmistakable summit of Golden Cap. The village of Charmouth hugs the hillside separated from Lyme Regis further west by the notorious unstable cliff of Black Venn.

Chesil Beach.

CHESIL BEACH

East from The Hive, stretching almost as far as the eye can see, for over 16 miles, is the vast shingle spit of Chesil Beach. The name is derived from the Saxon word for pebble being Chesil.

From Burton Bradstock the ridge is attached to the mainland, but beyond Abbotsbury the Fleet Lagoon separates it until reaching the north-western tip of Portland. The beach is made up of shingle that consists mainly of flint and chert. The pebbles are round and smooth and are graded from pea size on the western extent at Burton Bradstock to potato size at Portland.

Tradition has it that fishermen and smugglers landing on the beach in the dark of night could judge their exact location by the size of the pebbles.

The origin of the beach is subject to much debate. In 1853 it was thought to have been built from gravel driven along the shore, as part of the material is similar to that found at Budleigh Salterton in Devon. Another theory from 1975 suggested that it grew from the north of Portland with the grading of pebbles caused by motion along the shore.

Information on the beach provides the following theory due to rising sea levels that began at the end of the last Ice Age over 10,000 years ago. 'Chesil Beach was formed in the Holocene age which was approximately 6,000 years ago. It was formed by rising sea levels and it now protects the lowlands of Weymouth and the Fleet which is considered one of the most important lagoons in Europe. It is one of the finest barrier beaches in the world.'

The forming of the beach; 'Approximately 125,000 years ago, the sea levels were higher than they are today and landslides of East Devon and West Dorset were active. Then, during the Ice Age, sea levels dropped. The cliffs along this coastline decayed into large debris slopes that spilled across the exposed sea floor. When the Ice Age ended, the rising sea levels reached these large landslides and released vast amounts of chert and flint into the shoreline. Long shore drift then carried the pebbles eastward and covered the beach that was brought by the rising sea. The beach is still moving on shore.' (Jurassic Coast.)

Beware of strong tides and currents on Chesil Beach. Chesil Beach shelves steeply and there are no lifeguards, although Perry Buoys are provided along the beach.

Sunrise over Portland and the Fleet Lagoon.

Chesil Beach has, for as long as time can be remembered, been a hazard to shipping, for even on a fine summers day there seems to be a prevalent sea breeze that would have tempted many a sailing ship to run ashore. During south-westerly gales a wreck would almost be a certainty. Legend has it that the inhabitants of the coast at times would show lights in bad weather in the hope that it would cause a shipwreck, with the bounty of salvage their goal. The waves break with prodigious force creating a strong undertow, a constant danger to brave hearted swimmers and small craft.

During the 19th century the British army discovered that by bouncing cannon balls on water it increased their range. Barnes Wallis, an English scientist and engineer, began experimenting with skipping marbles over a tank of water in his garden. The idea of the bomb was that it would skim over the surface of the water and sink directly beneath the ship or up against a dam wall, with the force of the explosion concentrated by the surrounding water. The RAF accepted Wallis' theory and prototypes were tested at the National Physics Laboratory in Teddington. The tests proved successful and the real thing was tried out off Chesil Beach during December 1942.

The National Trust now owns a significant part of the beach between West Bay and Abbotsbury.

Writers have described Swyre as being, 'in a picturesque and rather privileged position near the coast of West Dorset'. At its heart is Holy Trinity Church, originally built in the early 16th century, far later than many other churches in the county. The plain unadorned building of which only the tower and the chancel arch remain from the original construction, was rebuilt during the 19th century, a time that witnessed much rebuilding of parish churches throughout the county.

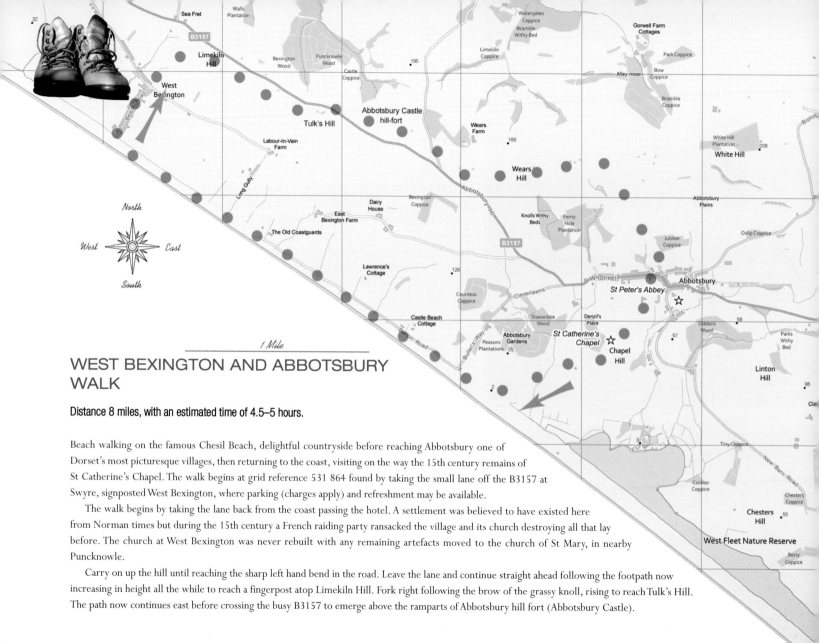

WEST BEXINGTON AND ABBOTSBURY WALK

Distance 8 miles, with an estimated time of 4.5–5 hours.

Beach walking on the famous Chesil Beach, delightful countryside before reaching Abbotsbury one of Dorset's most picturesque villages, then returning to the coast, visiting on the way the 15th century remains of St Catherine's Chapel. The walk begins at grid reference 531 864 found by taking the small lane off the B3157 at Swyre, signposted West Bexington, where parking (charges apply) and refreshment may be available.

The walk begins by taking the lane back from the coast passing the hotel. A settlement was believed to have existed here from Norman times but during the 15th century a French raiding party ransacked the village and its church destroying all that lay before. The church at West Bexington was never rebuilt with any remaining artefacts moved to the church of St Mary, in nearby Puncknowle.

Carry on up the hill until reaching the sharp left hand bend in the road. Leave the lane and continue straight ahead following the footpath now increasing in height all the while to reach a fingerpost atop Limekiln Hill. Fork right following the brow of the grassy knoll, rising to reach Tulk's Hill. The path now continues east before crossing the busy B3157 to emerge above the ramparts of Abbotsbury hill fort (Abbotsbury Castle).

Ordnance Survey data © Crown copyright and database right 2012

Turn right at the fingerpost atop Limekiln Hill, following the grassy brow rising to reach Tulk's Hill.

The Iron Age hill fort covers an area of 4 acres and had double ramparts with an outline of huts still visible. The fort was occupied by the Celtic Durotriges, a tribe living in Dorset, Wiltshire and Somerset prior to the Roman invasion. The strategic position of the hill fort placed it in the front line against invasion. When the Romans came in AD 43 it is said to have fallen quickly with the Romans marching onto Maiden Castle.

Past the triangulation pillar, you come to a quiet lane. Cross the lane then continue along the signposted inland coastal path. In just under a mile go through a gate and take the fork in the path to descend the hillside, heading all the while for the village of Abbotsbury.

Once on the small track, continue the descent to the village where you turn right onto Back Street, passing delightful cottages, to emerge close to the centre of the village. Ample options now present you with a choice of refreshment before the return to Chesil Beach.

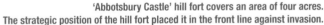

**'Abbotsbury Castle' hill fort covers an area of four acres.
The strategic position of the hill fort placed it in the front line against invasion.**

The South Dorset Ridgeway forms part of the South West Coast Path National Trail. The Ridgeway section of the trail runs for 17 miles from West Bexington to Osmington Mills.

Take Chapel Street, the small lane leading off left at the village stores, to follow the signposts directing you to the Swannery where you fork right to ascend the hillside to St Catherine's Chapel. The concluding part of the walk continues descending the hillside to rejoin the coast path heading in the direction of West Bexington.

   The walk back to West Bexington is now over the pebbled beach and in spring through to summer wild flowers burst into bloom among the pebbles with Sea Campion, Thrift (Sea Pinks) and Sea Kale dancing in the sea breezes. A good companion on this walk should be a wild flower book to enable identification of the many different species.

Trig point S5769. The standard design of the triangulation pillar was attributed to Brigadier Martin Hotine then head of the trigonometrical department at Ordnance Survey. No longer used, due to the development of aerial photography and GPS, some have been removed but many remain not least as an icon of the countryside but as a valuable reference point for walkers.

Continue along the beach, either taking the easier landward route or the more arduous but nevertheless pleasing seaward side, passing Lawrence's Cottage a former farmhouse built in the early mid 18th century of traditional rubble stone walls and thatched roof. From here it's a mile and a half back to the start.

During the 18th century smuggling was prolific along these shores as we have already discovered. One notorious smuggler, so the story goes, was Isaac Gulliver who owned a farm on Eggarton Hill, used for collecting and distributing his contraband. A report from the Custom House, Poole, to His Majesty's Commissioners of Customs in London in 1788 mentioned that: 'Gulliver was considered one of the greatest and most notorious smugglers in the west of England and particularly in the spirits and tea trade', it went onto mention him 'having vaults at various places along the coast and in remote places'.

The National Trust purchased land around West Bexington to help preserve the integrity of the pebble barrier, designated a Site of Special Scientific interest (SSSI) and an Area of Outstanding Natural Beauty (ANOB). The *Domesday Book* refers to the village as Bessintone, meaning village or farm.

Once refreshed, the journey now continues leaving West Bexington by the only road returning to Swyre where the B3157 travelling east will yield several opportunities to stop and admire the panorama of Chesil Beach and Portland before descending from the ridge once again to the historic village of Abbotsbury.

The walk exudes the pastoral delights of Dorset.

The vast expanse of Chesil Beach is your companion for the return to West Bexington.

Opposite: Abbotsbury retains the charm and atmosphere of a bygone era.

ABBOTSBURY

Set behind the Chesil bank, beneath the rolling Dorset hills, is the idyllic village of Abbotsbury, famous for its Swannery and Sub Tropical Gardens. Founded around the Fleet lagoon over 600 years ago, the Swannery has become one of Dorset's most popular attractions, established by Benedictine monks who built a monastery at Abbotsbury during the 11th century. Above the lagoon and overlooking the village is St Catherine's Chapel dating from the prosperous 15th century.

Evidence of prehistoric mans occupation of the area, dates from around 3000BC with a long barrow located north-east of the village, having a single burial chamber and originally roofed with a cap stone at its south-east entrance. Noted on the OS map as Grey Mare and her Colts, the site can be located at grid reference 583 870.

The Iron Age hill fort located north-west of Wears Hill is further evidence of the importance of the area with Dorset's most celebrated hill fort, Maiden Castle, situated less than 6 miles further east.

Signs of Roman occupation dates from the first century with discoveries of fragments of pottery and coins found throughout the area around Abbotsbury. At the time when the Romans retreated from Britain it is thought a church was first built in the settlement with the wooden structure suffering at the hands of Saxon raiders around AD 500.

During the 11th century King Canute rewarded the services of Orca with land in Abbotsbury. Orca and his wealthy wife Tola set about building the abbey. The abbey was destroyed in 1539 during the Dissolution of the Monasteries. Henry VIII set about disbanding the monasteries, priories, convents and friaries in England and Wales between 1536 and 1541 when he was made supreme head of the Church of England. Some of the ruins are still visible around the church of St Nicholas.

The archetypal cottages of Abbotsbury date back to at least the 16th century, having thatched roofs, and characteristically built of rubble stone, with distinctive red brick chimneys.

The first post boxes were introduced in Britain from 1853, some 13 years after the introduction of the first postage stamp, the 'Penny Black'. Prior to the introduction of postage stamps all mail had to be taken to the Post Office and the appropriate fee paid. The cipher on this post box dates installation during the reign of Queen Victoria.

The scene could be any time in the past, apart that is, from the neat row of television aerials.

The great Tithe Barn was built during the latter part of the 14th century and is the longest barn in England, measuring 272ft, and was spared during the Dissolution. The barn was used as a location in the film adaptation of Thomas Hardy's novel *Far From The Madding Crowd.*

The parish church of St Nicholas dates from the 14th century.

During the 18th century Abbotsbury was a settlement of farmers and fisherman with smuggling said to have been a prevalent occupation. The industrial revolution did not leave Abbotsbury untouched, with cottage industries flourishing that included basket making and rope making. By the late 19th century the village could boast a butcher, a baker, a boot maker, blacksmiths, wheelwrights, tailors and millers.

The village streets are bordered by rows of 'picture postcard' cottages some dating from the 16th century.

The magnificent Abbotsbury Sub Tropical Gardens cover 20 acres and are filled with rare and exotic plants from all over the world.

St Nicholas was built as the Parish Church of Abbotsbury, at the site of the Abbey Church of St Peter, in the late 14th century.

The archetypal cottages of Abbotsbury date back to at least the 16th century, having thatched roofs, and characteristically built of rubble stone, with distinctive red brick chimneys, helping the village retain the charm and atmosphere of a bygone era. Thankfully any new building or conversions must now blend in with the appealing architecture of the village.

St Catherine's Chapel, dating from the prosperous 15th century stands on the seaward side of Abbotsbury.

St Catherine's Chapel, dating from the prosperous 15th century stands on the seaward side of Abbotsbury, dominating the landscape for many distant miles. Built by the monks of Abbotsbury Abbey as a pilgrimage chapel, its isolated setting allowed the monks to withdraw from the monastery during Lent, for private prayer and meditation.

The chapel was dedicated to St Catherine of Alexandria. The stone vaulted roof is supported by heavily buttressed golden bluff limestone walls giving the chapel its distinctive appearance. The chapel stands on what is now known as Chapel Hill. Legend has it that St Catherine was the patron saint of spinsters and the ruins are said to have been frequently visited by women seeking a husband.

Overlooking the sea the chapel would almost certainly have become a beacon after the Dissolution, thereby preserving its structure.

Opposite: The stone vaulted roof is supported by heavily buttressed golden bluff limestone walls giving the chapel its distinctive appearance.

Sheep graze below Chapel Hill, helping to create an idyll of rural Dorset.

The Dorset fingerpost at Portesham.

The Dorset fingerpost is thought to be a unique design creating a character to the countryside. This style is said to resemble the London Underground sign with its horizontal bar through the middle of the roundel. The location and six figure grid reference around the bottom edge enables the location to be easily identified. A classic example can be found in the village of Portesham less than 2 miles from Chesil Beach. Portesham or, as would be pronounced in the true tradition of Dorset dialect, 'Possum' is another quintessential Dorset village with thatched stone cottages built around the church. The base of the tower of St Peter's is said to date from Norman times with most of the present building constructed during the 12th and 13th centuries.

The church of St Peter's is said to date from Norman times with most of the present building constructed during the 12th and 13th centuries.

The church is part of the Dorset Wildlife Trust's 'Living Churchyard' project managing the churchyard for the benefit of wildlife, at times leaving areas of grass uncut, allowing wild flowers to grow. This in turn encourages more insects, increasing the number of birds to the area. Snowdrops and violets in spring are followed by a constant supply of flowers throughout summer and into the autumn. The setting is enhanced by the delightful stream that babbles beside the church and the street.

Thomas Masterman Hardy lived in the village at Portesham House. Born in 1769 the son of Joseph Hardy he joined the navy in 1781 serving under Nelson before joining HMS *Victory* in 1803.

He died at Greenwich in 1839 and his memorial reads:

'The Friend and Companion-in-arms of Nelson. Eminent for judgement and self-possession. Ever anxious for the improvement of the service to which he had devoted himself. Equal to all its difficulties and duties, and conversant with its minutest details. The name of this gallant and distinguished officer will descend to posterity as one of the noblest ornaments of the profession to which England is so much indebted for security and renown.'

In 1885 the coming of the railways would reach Portesham, with the station on the branch line from Weymouth to Abbotsbury opening in September that year.

The line was set up by the local squire to transport shale oil as he understood there to be large quantities of mineral deposits on his land. Unfortunately for the squire that was not the case and the line remained as an uneconomic branch line. Passenger numbers increased briefly during the summer months with the attraction of the Swannery at Abbotsbury. This boosted the line but as befell the branch line at West Bay and throughout the country the increase in motor car ownership served to reduce passenger numbers even further.

The branch line became absorbed within the Great Western Railway but as the tourist trade diminished the line eventually closed in 1952. However, Dr Beeching cannot be held responsible for the closure as it was over a decade later that his infamous axe began to fall. Fortunately the station building remains, now a private residence.

St Peter's is set in the heart of the village beside a delightful stream.

High above the village the South Dorset Ridgeway runs parallel to the coast form Weymouth to Dorchester, with evidence of mans activity traced back to Neolithic times, with earthworks discovered dating back to 3600 BC. Several Bronze Age burials mounds are also evident. Such is the archaeological significance of the area, it is deemed to be as important as the World Heritage Sites of Stonehenge and Avebury. Close to Hardy's Monument is a cromlech, called Hell Stone, nine upright stones supporting a capstone, thought to have been the burial place of a Stone Age Chieftain. Local legend has it that the devil flung it from Portland as he was diverting himself at quoits.

The churchyard is home to many varieties of flowers during the spring through to late summer.

The tower of St Peter's Church.

HARDY IN DORSET

The name Hardy has at times caused confusion in Dorset.

Thomas Hardy, the author and poet, was born at Higher Bockhampton, a hamlet to the east of Dorchester on 2 June 1840. His father Thomas was a stonemason with his mother Jemima being well read. Thomas' early education was provided by his mother and it was from her he gained an appetite for learning and a desire for the delights of the Dorset countryside. University was well beyond the means of his family and his education ceased at the age of 16, to become an apprentice architect. On moving to London in 1862 he enrolled as a student at King's College. It was said that he never felt at home in London: conscious of the class divide due to his social standing. Concerns over his health saw him return to Dorset in 1867, deciding to dedicate his time to writing.

The manuscript of Hardy's first novel *The Poor Man and The Lady* in 1867 was destroyed as he failed to find a publisher for the work. Persuaded to write again he set about writing *Under The Greenwood Tree* and *Desperate Remedies* both published anonymously in 1871 but importantly incorporating real places in Dorset, within the plots. *Under The Greenwood Tree* brought acclaim to the writer for the first time. In 1873 he published *A Pair of Blue Eyes* under his own name, said to have been about his courtship with his first wife.

Far From The Madding Crowd published in 1874 was set in Puddletown, a village near his birthplace, with the novel becoming a great success allowing him to take up his literary career full time. The next 25 years would see a further 10 novels published.

The Hardy's moved to London but soon returned to Dorset to live for a time in Sturminster Newton where he wrote *Return of The Native* said to be one of his most enduring works. 1885 saw a move to Dorchester where his architectural skills helped him design a new home, Max Gate. Within a year he had published *The Mayor of Casterbridge* followed by *The Woodlanders* in 1887.

Towards the end of the century he concentrated on poetry partly because of his disillusionment with society surrounding the morality of his novels *Tess of the d'Urbervilles* and *Jude the Obscure* published in 1896.

Thomas Hardy died on 11 January 1928 and is buried at Westminster Abbey. However, he had expressed the wish to be buried beside Emma, his first wife. His wishes were only partly regarded as his body was interred in Poet's Corner, Westminster Abbey, his heart though, it is said, was buried in Emma's grave at Stinsford.

The monument high on the Blackdown Hills was erected by public subscription in 1844 and has recently undergone major restoration works.

High on the summit of Blackdown Hill above the village of Portesham, less than 5 miles west from Dorchester and 8 miles distance from Hardy's cottage, is Hardy Monument, and this is where visitors may be forgiven if they assume that the monument was built in memory of the life and times of the author and poet Thomas Hardy. The monument was erected in honour of Sir Thomas Masterman Hardy who we have discovered lived in Portesham until 1781 before joining the Navy. Hardy was the flag captain, the captain of Nelson's Flagship HMS *Victory* at the Battle of Trafalgar and the immortal words are probably known to most that were spoken as the two stood on the deck in a moment of triumph, when Nelson was hit by a musket ball from a French vessel. 'They have done me at last' said Nelson and he was taken below. Nelson's last words were described as saying 'Take care of my dear Lady Hamilton, Hardy, take care of poor Lady Hamilton'. He paused then said very faintly, 'Kiss me, Hardy'. This, Hardy did, on the cheek. Nelson then said, 'Now I am satisfied. Thank God I have done my duty'.

The monument's location is enhanced as the early morning sun rises over the pastoral Dorset countryside and the Isle of Portland

Built of Portland stone, the monument affords distant views to the Solent and The Needles off the Isle of Wight visible on a clear day. The monument stands 72ft high, set at its vantage point over 780ft above sea level.

THE PROPERTY OF THE
NATIONAL
TRUST

ERECTED BY PUBLIC SUBSCRIPTION IN THE YEAR 1844
IN MEMORY OF
VICE ADMIRAL SIR THOMAS MASTERMAN HARDY BART. G.C.B.
FLAG CAPTAIN TO LORD NELSON
ON H M S VICTORY AT THE BATTLE OF TRAFALGAR
RESTORED 1900
AND PLACED IN CHARGE OF THE NATIONAL TRUST
FOR PLACES OF HISTORIC INTEREST OR NATURAL BEAUTY
BY THE DESCENDANTS OF SIR THOMAS MASTERMAN HARDY
ON WHOSE LAND IT STANDS

The style is said to resemble the London Underground sign with its horizontal bar through the middle of the roundel. The location and six figure grid reference around the bottom edge enables the location to be easily identified.

FINGERPOSTS

In 1697 legislation was passed enabling local magistrates to erect direction posts at cross highways, but it was the highways act of 1773 that made it compulsory to erect fingerposts on turnpike roads.

More than a century later the motor car act of 1903 passed responsibility of road signs to the relevant highway authority with guidance detailing that the lettering should be all upper case and written on a white background, with the name of the highway authority included.

Old Fleet Church, all that remains of the church at East Fleet.

FLEET

The village of Fleet lies 4 miles south-east of Abbotsbury close to the lagoon from which it takes its name. In 1824 a tremendous storm and tumultuous seas caused severe damage and flooding to many places along Chesil Beach. Many parts of the village were destroyed by the storm, including what is now the old Fleet Church. The wind was said to have been so intense, and the sea so heavy, that it caused the waves to crash over Chesil Beach swamping the village in its path. Although part of the church in East Fleet was destroyed, the chancel remains, standing within sight of the sea, an everlasting accolade to those who built it, and a reminder of the potent force of the sea that destroyed it. The interior is well cared for with a few grave stones to be seen in the churchyard.

The church and its vault features in J. Meade Faulkner's 1898 novel, *Moonfleet.*

The inside of old Fleet Church.

The new church of Holy Trinity was completed in 1829. Fleet is a beautiful, tranquil corner of Dorset more akin to a hamlet than a village, its history does, however, include the darker tales of smuggling and was featured in the novel *Moonfleet* by J. Meade Falkner first published in 1898.

Moonfleet is set in 1757 in a small village in Dorset close to the sea. John Trenchard, a young orphan boy, lives in the village of Moonfleet with his aunt and discovers a vault at the local church. Unwittingly he finds himself in a smugglers den and eventually becomes drawn into their dealings. What follows is an amazing adventure, what will be the outcome between the smugglers and the revenue men? Blackbeard's diamond, reputed to have been stolen from King Charles I, is discovered and John and his father-figure leave the village to undertake many adventures. Tales of smuggling, guns, thieves and romance follow. *Moonfleet* today is still a popular book and has often been studied in many schools as part of the curriculum.

The legends of smugglers has in the modern day conjured up a world of romance and idyll but in reality it was a brutal world, where it is said the contraband would be protected at all cost. The Lords of the manor and even the vicar could well have been collaborators of the smugglers, indeed even some of the customs officers would turn a blind eye to what was going on. The first verse of *The Smugglers Song* echoes the reality of smuggling and is taken from *Puck of Pook's Hill* by Rudyard Kipling first published in 1906.

If you wake at midnight, and hear a horse's feet,
Don't go drawing back the blind, or looking in the street.
Them that ask no questions isn't told a lie.
Watch the wall, my darling, while the Gentlemen go by!
Five and twenty ponies,
Trotting through the dark -
Brandy for the Parson,
'Baccy for the Clerk;
Laces for a lady, letters for a spy,
And watch the wall, my darling, while the Gentlemen go by!

Opposite: All that remains today is a tiny church, with a few gravestones in the churchyard.

The cottages of Butter Street lead down to Fleet Old Church.

Butter Street is the delightful row of cottages leading down to Fleet Old Church. The original end cottage was demolished due to the storm in 1824. An account of the storm is detailed in *The Story of Fleet and its Old Church*, a booklet available in the tiny church compiled by Revd O.J. Newman and Mrs Edwards-Stuart in 1986. George Bowering, the Parish Clerk of Fleet, remembered his father James Bowering describing the scene as a lad aged 11. 'The sea began to break over the beach at 5am, the water came up as fast as a horse could gallop. James watched as long as he dared, and then, terrified, ran for his life to Chickerell. The nave of the church was undermined and demolished, also a cottage hard by and another at the end of Butter Street. Two cottages near the garden of the old Priest's house were also thrown down. Two old ladies living in the Priest's house were rescued from a bedroom window. A hayrick was swept away and seven large fishing boats were washed inland.'

Building of the new church began in 1826 and was completed in 1829. The church was dedicated to the Holy Trinity in 1829. Some of the relics recovered from the remains of the old church were placed in the new one, including the old church bell, said to peal out its continuing message.

The waters of the fleet are 'brackish', being neither fresh nor not as salty as sea water.

FLEET LAGOON

Cut off from the sea for most of its eight miles the lagoons only influence from salt water, aside from storms that can at times cause sea water to surge through the shingle, is a narrow channel at Ferry Bridge. With each tide the eastern part of the lagoon is subjected to strong currents with the salt water ebbing and flowing. Further west the lagoon widens and the salt water is dispersed, mixing with the fresh water from several small rivers that drain into the lagoon near to Langdon Herring and Abbotsbury, producing brackish water. The shallow waters of the lagoon are warmer than the sea in the summer months, but cooler during the winter months, the effect heightened at the western end. The lagoon covers an area of 480 hectares.

The classic view from the Isle of Portland at grid reference 687 729 almost 400ft above sea level, looking north-west, taking in the entire shingle spit of Chesil Beach.

Trinity House had built two new lighthouses at Portland Bill in 1869 with the present single tower superseding them, completed in 1906.

Beyond the villages of East and West Fleet and Chickerell the main road passes through the village of Wyke Regis on our journey to Portland Bill, although the area is perhaps described more so today as a suburb of Weymouth. The history of the area can be traced back to the Stone Age with hand axes having been discovered along the Fleet.

The village church of All Saints served Weymouth up until the 19th century. Although earlier structures were built on this site the present church was consecrated in 1455, constructed using local stone from Portland. King George III attended All Saints while visiting during the summers between 1790 and 1805.

The victims of the wreck of the *Earl of Abergavenny* including the captain John Wordsworth, brother of poet William Wordsworth, are buried in the churchyard. In February 1805 a small fleet of Indiamen set sail on an 18-month voyage from Portsmouth to Bengal and China. Included in the fleet on her fifth voyage was the 1,440 tonne *Earl of Abergavenny*, built in 1797 to carry cargo for the British East India Company.

A short time into the voyage with adverse weather conditions and much confusion, the Earl struck the Shambles sandbank off the southern tip of Portland Bill. Although the crew managed to clear the bank the ship was badly damaged, so much so that she sank on 5 February while heading for the safety of Weymouth. Over 250 souls perished that bitterly cold night by drowning or exposure, a tremendous loss of life from a total number on board of 402. She still lies today, in 60ft of water, less than 2 miles from the beach in Weymouth Bay.

PORTLAND BILL

A lighthouse at Portland Bill was established in 1716 by William Holman, who having gained the support of ship-owners of Weymouth, put forward a petition to Trinity House. The scheme met with opposition as had a previous plan as early as 1669. There were originally two lighthouses with enclosed lanterns and coal fires. The upkeep of the lights was somewhat less than effective and Trinity House engaged William Johns, a local builder, to erect a new lighthouse, the light beginning operation in 1789. The area around Portland Bill is treacherous to vessels, with many succumbing to the Portland Race, caused by the tides between the Bill and the Shambles sandbank, lying 3 miles off shore.

Portland has for many centuries seen its stone quarried for building material and evidence of this activity can still be seen. At Portland Bill the maze of 'beach' huts huddled around the lighthouse have been described as a 'holiday home shanty town', part of their charm emanating in their haphazard layout, in stark contrast to the regimental rows traditionally along the seafront of many of Dorset's beaches.

The lectern known as Pulpit Rock was formed by quarrymen in the 1870s after a natural arch was cut away.

The effect of this disturbance can easily be seen from the shore. The lighthouse was set to guide vessels through these treacherous waters and act as a way mark for ships navigating the English Channel.

The lighthouse at Portland was the first in England to be lit by Argand lamps, invented and patented in 1780 by Aime Argand, a Swiss physicist. The light was a great improvement on the home oil lamp of the time, producing a light equivalent to 10 candles. During the French Revolution two cannons were installed in the tower.

Trinity House built two new lighthouses in 1869 with the present single tower superseding them, completed in 1906. The old higher and lower towers are still in place as is the 23ft white stone obelisk, built in 1844 at the southern tip of Portland Bill, as a warning of the low shelf of rock extending south, into the sea.

The existing lighthouse was fully automated in 1996, with monitoring of the light transferred to Trinity House Operations Centre in Harwich, Essex.

The lighthouse stands 136ft high. The round sandstone tower is painted white with a single broad red band at its centre, with the keepers house adjoining. Today it is used as a visitor centre. The lighthouse's characteristic flash is said to be most unusual, due to the arrangement of the panels. The character gradually changes from one flash to four flashes, between the bearings 221° and 224° and from four flashes to one flash, between bearings 117° and 141°.

The lighthouse stands 136ft high with the keepers house adjoining. Today it is used as a visitor centre, during the summer, and has a display depicting Trinity House lighthouses and shipwrecks.

A 23ft white stone obelisk, built in 1844, at the southern tip of Portland Bill warns of the low shelf of rock extending south into the sea.

Early mariners were guided by fires built atop a hill, their main function was, however, as an entrance marker, rather than warning of rocks or treacherous conditions. By placing the fire on a platform it would improve visibility and lead to the development of the lighthouse.

The visitor centre at Portland Bill is open during the summer, and has a display depicting Trinity House lighthouses and shipwrecks.

The old lower tower built in 1869 and upper tower are still in place, superseded by the new lighthouse in 1906.

The Island has for many centuries seen its stone quarried for building material. The Palace of Westminster 1347, the Tower of London 1349 and Exeter Cathedral are all prime examples of 14th-century craftsmanship using Portland stone. Perhaps one of the most famous is St Paul's Cathedral, rebuilt by Sir Christopher Wren following the great fire of London in 1666. The stone was transported by sailing barges from Portland to the centre of London making use of the Thames. Many other churches in the capital were also rebuilt using what was described as the finest of stone. In the USA the United Nations building has been partly built in Portland stone as well as many other famous buildings across the world.

Portland was more noted for agriculture than quarrying in mediaeval times, with the *Domesday Book* recording that it was inhabited by farmers and fishermen, with 900 sheep on the island. By 1840 the Portland sheep had reached record numbers of 4,000 but their decline came with the increase in quarrying for the valuable stone, and the inevitable increase for housing needs.

Tradition has it that Thomas Hardy refers to Portland as 'The Isle of Slingers', due to the islanders throwing stones to keep strangers away.

Portland is of course not an island but, geographically speaking, a peninsula a word derived from Latin, 'pene' meaning almost and 'insula' meaning island. Portland's terrain is, in the main, craggy with dramatic rock structures and is strategically positioned in the English Channel, barely attached to the mainland by Chesil Beach and a small section of land.

PORTLAND HARBOUR

Portland Harbour is now a popular venue for sailing, wind surfing and diving, and the venue for sailing events during the 2012 Olympic games. The present harbour began life in 1849 when the Royal Navy constructed a breakwater to the south using blocks of Portland stone from local quarries. Two further breakwaters were added in 1906 to alleviate the threat of torpedo attacks. In 1914, at the commencement of hostilities, HMS *Hood* was sunk as a block ship to fill a hole in the breakwater. Her hulk was to serve as a barrier to prevent German U-boats from firing torpedoes into the harbour. She remains in the same position to this day. As well as a leisure facility the harbour is used by commercial ships including bulk tankers and container carriers with the occasional cruise ship calling into port, bringing visitors to the Dorset coast.

WEYMOUTH

The town of Weymouth developed during the 12th century, originally at what is now Wyke Regis. By the middle of the 13th century it had become established as a seaport. The borough of Melcombe Regis developed to the north of the harbour and is infamously associated with being the first port at which the Black Death came into England in 1348.

The Black Death was one of the most devastating pandemics in history reaching Europe in 1348. Believed to have originated from China, the disease would have travelled along the Silk Road, spread by the fleas from black rats that were often unwelcome passengers aboard merchant ships. The villages and hamlets on the outskirts of Weymouth would soon fall victim to the Black Death causing occupants to seek refuge inland. As they did the bubonic plague swept through southern England like a raging forest fire. The Black Death took two forms, one that would result in death within the hour of the first symptom of haemorrhaging. The second would manifest as great black swellings under the arms and groin that lasted a couple of days, then death followed, although a few survived taking many months to recover.

Weymouth and Melcombe Regis were rival ports until a Royal Charter was granted by Elizabeth I to unite the boroughs as Weymouth and Melcombe Regis. Weymouth taking its name from the River Wey. A spring rises next to a wishing well in the village of Upwey some 3 miles north of Weymouth with the upper reaches of the river very picturesque. The shallow brook meanders through the valley before continuing on its journey to reach the sea. The villages of Upwey, Broadwey, Chickerell, Radipole and Littlemoor have now become part of the built up area.

The port has witnessed many historical sailings from within its harbour walls, including the departure of Captain Richard Clarke, discovering Newfoundland, with trade links then established within the town. A fleet of ships left Weymouth to meet the Spanish Armada in 1588, in total over 200 local men set sail. During the early 17th century Weymouth was the departure port for some of the first ships sailing to America.

King George III who had visited Weymouth in 1789 made use of the earliest bathing machines. His visits were commemorated by a monument built on the sea front in recognition of his Golden Jubilee, with a chalk figure carved in the hillside above Osmington, said to represent the King.

The Victorian age of railway building finally came to Weymouth in 1857 with the opening of the southern terminus of the Great Western Railway, creating a through route from Castle Cary in Somerset.

The clock was erected in 1887 to mark the 50th year of the reign of Queen Victoria. The clock was built on a stone base on the beach. The clock still stands in its original position but now stands proudly on the extended esplanade.

The late 19th-century shelters are an iconic feature of Weymouth seafront.

The distinctive esplanade railings with the Georgian seafront, built when the first tourists arrived, over 200 years ago.

The clock was originally set on a stone base on the sands. During the 1920s the esplanade was built to protect the beach from erosion.

PUNCH & JUDY

The origins of Punch & Judy in Britain can be traced back to the mid-17th century, a regular sight witnessed in most major cities throughout the country. The earliest written account was by Samuel Pepys who wrote in 1662 on a visit to Covent Garden 'Thence to see an Italian puppet play that is within the rails there, which is very pretty, the best that ever I saw, and great resort of gallants'. It is said Pepys returned many times and continued to be amused.

It was, however, during the middle part of the 19th century that Punch was first seen at the seaside, in the main due to the advent of the railways allowing the wealthy to take day trips to the coastline of Britain – and Weymouth was no exception. The popularity of a visit to the seaside was boosted by the introduction of bank holidays in 1871, with travel to the coast now becoming more affordable for many families, heightening the popularity of Punch & Judy.

Punch & Judy has stayed popular down the centuries not least for maintaining a topical theme. Punch would fight and beat Hitler and in more recent times, Punch has faced up to famous politicians.

The shows have always been busked and Weymouth is probably the very last resort in England that has had a continuous run (apart from the war years) of Punch & Judy on its beach. Professors Murray, Staddon, Edmonds and Higgins have all performed their unique interpretation and today the tradition is continued by Professor Mark Poulton. Mark took over the reins from Professor Guy Higgins in 2005, his predecessor performing at Weymouth since 1976.

The performances constantly change and the professor makes all of the puppets. In 2009 Weymouth presented Professor Poulton and Mr Punch to Her Majesty the Queen and HRH the Duke of Edinburgh Prince Philip.

Professor Poulton's fame has spread far beyond Weymouth, with television appearances on the BBC's *Countryfile* programme with John Craven, and a cameo appearance on the television documentary, *Edwardian Farm* in 2010.

The professor makes all the puppets.

SAND SCULPTURES AND SANDWORLD

Sculptures in Sand can be found on the seafront at the far end of Weymouth town centre near the beach amusements. Sculptures in Sand, was started by F.G. Darrington, whose passion for sand sculpting began just after World War One in the early 1920s. This was before the quay extensions to Weymouth Harbour had been built. The tide used to run up to the promenade as the level of the beach was lower than it is today. Fred would jump down when the tide went out and draw grand castles and cathedrals in the sand for the public to admire. The onlookers would throw coins onto the sand to show their appreciation. As the tide came back in the coins would be thrown into the sea. Fred would dive in and retrieve them to the delight of the crowd.

Fred was one of a number of lads running this sort of attraction during the summer. Fred started sand sculpting in the 1920s which proved to be an even greater attraction. A lad called Swift Vincent also began sand sculpting on Weymouth Beach at this time. Fred's skills improved and refined until he became one of the world's acknowledged masters of sand sculpting. Fred was entirely self-taught and he worked from the 1920s right up until 1996 when he retired at the age of 86.

Mark Anderson, Fred's grandson, is the present sand sculptor. Mark helped his grandfather from the age of 11. At first he ran errands and made the tea, also learning how to mix the sand and water binding it together ready for sand sculpting. He then became an apprentice in 1988 at the age of 22.

Mark had to develop his own skills. Fred never told him what to do but was always there for tips and advice. Mark had to serve his apprenticeship in front of the crowds, and progressed quickly to avoid the forthright observations of the younger members of the audience. Mark knew he had succeeded when he turned up for work one day to find Fred had changed the sign to 'Sand Sculptures by F.G. Darrington & Grandson'. Mark was very proud and today he runs Sculptures in Sand on his own but ever mindful of the influence of his kindly grandfather.

Incredible sand sculptures ranging from two up to five metres high are the focus of Sandworld at Lodmoor Country Park. All the sculptures are made from 100 per cent pure sand by competing World Class International Sand Artists. The main sculptures are showcased under cover in a huge marquee.

A sand sculpture is a construction made only of sand and water. It could be a sand castle, but it could also be a composition of other architectural forms, people or animals and objects. Using the right sand and the right techniques, nearly any shape can be created. Sand sculpture is an art form which was already used by the Egyptians in 4000 BC.

These images of the sculptures created at Sandworld by a team of international sand artists depict old man of the sea, Neptune and pirates. The team led by Mark Anderson were put together to create Weymouth's newest, and amazing, all weather visitor attraction.

Travel and in particular the railways, were an important development during the reign of Queen Victoria allowing goods and passengers to be transported rapidly.

It was during the Victorian era that standard railway time was introduced. Throughout the early 19th century time was determined in each town known as local mean time, which until the coming of the railways was not a concern, as travel between towns would take several hours and on longer journeys sometimes days to complete.

The time difference varied by up to 20 minutes from London time, with Bristol being 10 minutes behind, this time difference evolved due to the sun setting later the further west you travel from London. It soon became apparent that even such small discrepancies in times caused confusion for travellers, and railway time was applied, initially by the Great Western Railway in 1840. This move was soon followed by other railway companies throughout Britain. London time was set at Greenwich with railway clocks having two minute hands displaying both local and railway time.

The time set at Greenwich by the Royal Observatory was eventually adopted as standard time in 1880 becoming known as Greenwich Mean Time, GMT.

Weymouth and Portland Borough Council provide berths for over 450 vessels at their two marinas in the inner harbour.

The *Pelican* is a sailing ship originally built in France in 1946.

The lobster pot, a traditional feature on a harbour side.

The first bridge linking the ports of Weymouth and Melcombe Regis dates from 1597 with the present structure built in 1930, operating on the same design as Tower Bridge in London.

Town Bridge, completed in 1930, was built to replace an earlier structure dating from 1824. The new bridge is a bascule bridge, designed to lift up, similar to Tower Bridge in London, to allow the safe passage of larger ships in and out of the harbour.

Perhaps, the most iconic feature that stands out on Weymouth's seafront, has to be the Jubilee clock. For generations it's been used as a meeting point and a beacon should children become lost among the many sun worshippers on the beach during balmy summer days. The clock was erected in 1887 to mark the 50th year of Queen Victoria's reign, set on a stone base on the sands. During the 1920s the esplanade was built to protect the sands from the encroachment of shingle from the eastern end of the beach toward Bowleaze Cove.

Rock pools can be explored at low tide with the small pier dividing the beach near to where the River Jordan flows into the sea.

BOWLEAZE COVE

As we continue ever east, the Lodmoor RSPB nature reserve can be found on the low lying land between Weymouth and Bowleaze Cove. The large area of open water, salt marsh and reed beds attract many different birds and is designated a Site of Special Scientific Interest (SSSI).

Bowleaze Cove lies north-east of Weymouth and has been a favourite family holiday destination for many decades. Set close to the village of Preston where the golden sands of Weymouth have merged with Dorset shingle to provide a quiet, sheltered bay, complete with a slipway for the launching of small boats. The beach is a delightful combination of shell, shingle and sand with numerous rock pools at its eastern end. The River Jordon enters the sea at Bowleaze Cove rising as a spring close to the village of Sutton Poyntz.

John Constable visited Osmington on his honeymoon in October 1816 and he was inspired to paint *Weymouth Bay*, the scene looking west showing the small Jordon River flowing over the sands and Jordon Hill behind. The painting now hangs in the National Gallery, London.

In 1816 the leading English landscape artist John Constable spent his honeymoon at nearby Osmington Mills, where he was inspired to paint *Weymouth Bay*, represented by Bowleaze Cove, the painting now hangs in the National Gallery, London.

An iconic feature of Bowleaze Cove is the Grade II listed, Spanish Style Riviera Hotel. Built in the 1940s, it was formerly part of the Pontins holiday group from the late 1950s through to the late 1990s.

The Isle of Portland and its harbour lies due south from Bowleaze Cove, seen here across a silvery sea.

The Osmington White Horse was created in 1808 as a tribute to King George III, a regular visitor to his residence in Weymouth.

The South West Coast Path from Bowleaze Cove follows atop the comparatively low cliffs of Redcliff Point and Black Head, seen here from Osmington Mills.

OSMINGTON MILLS

Below the chalky figure of King George III, said to be the only chalk carving of a horse and rider in Britain, we find a winding country lane leading down to the cliff top. Set overlooking the sea in its own valley is the most idyllic location for the home of the 13th-century Smugglers Inn at Osmington Mills.

The inn, as its name suggests, was once home to smuggling and in particular the most notorious of smugglers in the area, Emmanual Charles. During the 19th century when he operated it was known as the Crown Inn, for obvious reasons no doubt. A coastguard house was built in 1835 some 13 years after the introduction of the coastguard service, positioned as it was with a view of both the back and front doors of the inn. The population of the tiny hamlet would have been dependent on fishing for their livelihoods but their incomes would have no doubt been subsidised by smuggling.

The parish church in Osmington is dedicated to St Osmund and dates from the early 12th century with additions during the 14th century and the tower built during the prosperous 15th century, a time that saw many church towers constructed throughout the country. The vicarage was home to John Constable for three months in 1816, a stay that resulted in the painting of *Weymouth Bay*.

The most noticeable features on the beach are the large rounded brown boulders. These huge boulders of carbonate-cemented sandstone are rounded with a division, giving a character that has been described as 'looking like a giant bun'. These huge boulders can be found in the layer of Bencliff grit formation at the base of the cliffs and gradually fall free, from the effects of wave action and weathering.

The rocks at the foot of the cliffs below Osmington exhibit remarkable colourful patterns.

These huge boulders, as large as a meter diameter, can be found in layers at the base of the cliffs. Weathering and wave action cause them to fall free, nearly spherical in shape with a part division along the equator.

White Nothe. A smugglers path begins from the beach at Ringstead Bay and zigzags up White Nothe with a particularly steep section near the top. The path featured as an escape route in the novel *Moonfleet*.

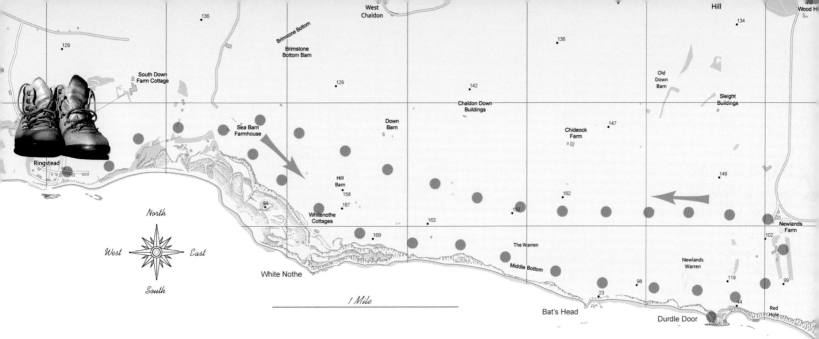

RINGSTEAD BAY TO DURDLE DOOR WALK

Distance 8 miles, with an estimated time of 4.5–5.5 hours.

Green fields, rugged chalk cliffs and pebbled beaches dominate this stretch of the coast. The first part of the route leads to one of the most photographed locations in Dorset, the magnificent arch of Durdle Door.

The distance, although not great, should not be underestimated as the walk necessitates several steep ascents and descents of the chalky cliff tops that are punctuated by dry valleys such as Scratchy Bottom, behind Durdle Door.

Just a few miles further east of Osmington Mills is the tiny settlement of Ringstead and the delightful cove of Ringstead Bay. The hamlet is only accessible by using the toll road (currently £5) giving use of the car park near the sea. Alternative parking is at the National Trust car park above South Down Farm. The beach at Ringstead is pebbled with some areas of sand. The original village and its church are documented in the *Domesday Book* but no longer exist, its location was inland to the west of the current settlement. One theory suggesting that it fell victim to the plague, being only a short distance from Melcombe Regis, while others believe it was at the hands of marauders, as befell West Bexington.

To the east of the bay the white chalk cliffs of White Nothe rise high, its inaccessible undercliff providing a secluded wildlife habitat. The cliffs were formed during the Cretaceous era 146 to 65 million years ago and are much younger than those found further west from the Jurassic era above Lyme Bay, creating a striking divide. The pure white chalk is made up of the skeletons of millions of sea algae and micro organisms.

The walk begins at grid reference 751 814 at the car park in Ringstead village.

The chalk headland between White Nothe and Swyre Head is known as Bat's Head. A new natural arch is in the early stages of formation in the chalk cliffs, known as Bat's Hole.

From Ringstead Bay a spectacular zigzag path climbs the cliff, believed to have been one of the locations used in the book *Moonfleet Bay*. However, our route takes us from the car park, heading towards the sea to join the track bearing left passing some cottages and a small caravan site. Bear left again along an enclosed track following woodland on the seaward side while steadily gaining height. During 1887–1915 the vicar of Stroud Green used Holworth House for holidays. His widow built a small church out of wood after selling Holworth House in 1926 and St Catherine-by-the-Sea, Holworth remains today in its delightful setting below Burning Cliff.

The cliff is so named from events during 1826 when part of the cliff slipped towards the sea, the landslip causing trapped oil and gas to ignite. The oil and gas was reported to have burnt for three years. The ascent now begins to quicken as the cliff top of White Nothe comes into view. The name it is said comes from the nose like shape of the chalk.

The views west to the Isle of Portland are awe inspiring, with a panorama opening up east as the route descends to Bats Head before climbing once again to reach Swyres Head. The path at times follows close to the edge of the chalk cliffs and great care should be taken on this part of the walk, particularly on the very steep gradients.

The spectacular formation of Durdle Door is now in view. The path now descends to Scratchy Bottom, a dry cliff top valley surrounded by farmland. Scratchy Bottom was used as the location of the opening scenes of the 1967 film *Far From The Madding Crowd* in which Gabriel Oak's sheep are driven over a cliff by his sheepdog.

The natural limestone arch of Durdle Door.

Scratchy Bottom is a dry valley above the chalk cliffs that rise behind Durdle Door. The valley was used as a location in the 1967 film *Far From The Madding Crowd*. Quite how its name originated is still a mystery. The name is thought to have derived from rough hollow, although other suggestions must have come to the fore.

The true spectacle of this iconic Dorset phenomenon unfolds as the path edges nearer, descending all the while, to one of the most photographed landmarks on the Jurassic Coast.

The route down to the beach necessitates tackling 150 steps although somewhat more arduous on the way back to the cliff top. There are no refreshments or toilets on the beach but public toilets are available at Durdle Door Holiday Park, and in summer refreshments may also be found.

Perhaps one of Dorset's most identifiable features, the limestone arch of Durdle Door.

Looking west from Durdle Door beach back to the chalk cliffs of Bat's Head, and beyond, the bustling resort of Weymouth can be seen shimmering in the distance.

The rock formation was a result of the softer rocks becoming eroded away behind the hard limestone rocks, allowing the sea to punch through. The beach has been used for many music, film and television locations including the film adaptation of Thomas Hardy's novel *Far From The Madding Crowd*.

Now at the halfway stage, the walk rejoins the coast path continuing east, for a while skirting the western edge of St Oswald's Bay, known locally as 'Man of War Bay'. The path then begins to rise inland passing through a car park before continuing downwards through the Holiday Park.

The arch silhouetted in the early morning light set against a restless sea.

St Oswald's Bay is known locally as Man of War Bay.

Once through the Holiday Park, take the path on the left at Newlands Farm now heading west along a bridal way and track. Three miles of easier ridge walking lie ahead until reaching farm buildings above Ringstead Bay. Take the track on your left descending Burning Cliff to rejoin the outward part of the route passing St Catherine-by-the-Sea, Holworth for the last mile back to Ringstead Village car park.

A short distance east of Durdle Door is the world renowned Lulworth Cove, however, due to the topography of the area it requires an 11 mile journey by road passing through the enchantingly named villages of Owermoigne and Winfrith Newburgh. Lying three miles inland, Owermoigne was a hive for smugglers with contraband hidden in the church. The rectory is said to have had a window, now blocked up, where once the rector's barrel would have been smuggled in. The tower used by the smugglers in the 18th century is the only part remaining of the church, dating originally from the 15th century; the remainder rebuilt in the late 1800s.

In the early 1800s Durdle Door appears on Ordnance Survey maps as, Dirdale Door. One theory suggests the name to have been derived from the Old English thyrelod 'pierced' with duru 'door'.

WINFRITH NEWBURGH

Mentioned in the *Domesday Book* as Winfrode, Winfrith Newburgh takes its name from the river that runs through the village. The village was originally on the ancient road from Dorchester to Wareham before a turnpike road was built, now the site of the A352.

Winfrith, as it is locally known, was the scene of an initially peaceful protest by agricultural workers in 1830. Agricultural workers felt their livelihoods were being threatened with low pay and, with the introduction of horse-powered threshing machines taking the jobs of several men, it was seen as the last straw. The Riot Act was read by the local magistrate but the protesters failed to disperse with three of them arrested. In 1832 six agricultural workers from Tollpuddle eight miles north of Winfrith formed a Friendly Society and began a renewed protest against these issues. They swore a secret oath and refused to work for less than 10 shillings a week.

James Frampton who had read the Riot Act at Winfrith invoked an obscure law against oath-swearing to prosecute those who became known as the Tollpuddle Martyrs. The six men were arrested and transported to Australia. A monument was erected in their honour in Tollpuddle in 1934, and a sculpture of the martyrs stands in the village in front of the Tollpuddle Martyrs Museum.

On leaving the village continue on the minor road, passing a turning to Durdle Door, to reach the village of West Lulworth and Lulworth Cove.

The village was originally on the ancient road from Dorchester to Wareham before a turnpike road was built.

The shape of Lulworth Cove is due to wave diffraction, the narrow entrance forcing the waves to spread out as they run to shore.

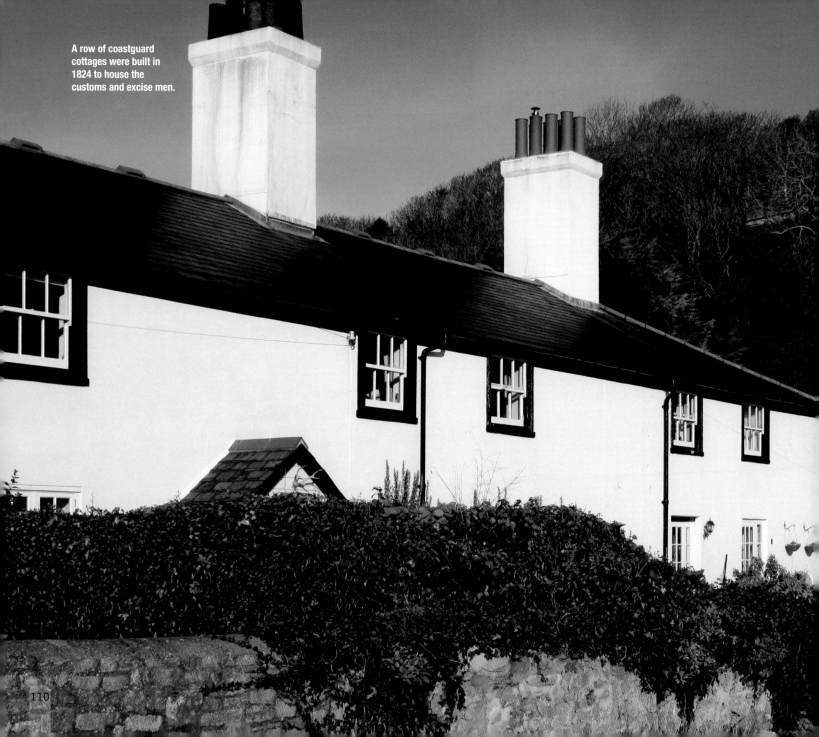

A row of coastguard cottages were built in 1824 to house the customs and excise men.

LULWORTH COVE

The world famous cove that needs no introduction was formed by the erosive powers of the sea. The cove was formed due to the alternating bands of rock running parallel to the shore. The rocks on the seaward side were made of clay and sand and have been eroded away with a narrow band of more resistant Portland limestone forming the shoreline. A band of less resistant Purbeck limestone is backed by a band of much less resistant greensand and clay. The back of the cove is formed of chalk which is more resilient than clay but not as resilient as the limestone.

The theory is that glacial melt waters would have eroded a hole in the hard Portland limestone forming the original cliff face, allowing the sea to enter. Once breached, the much softer rocks behind were eroded, creating the rounded cove. The shape of the cove is due to wave diffraction, the narrow entrance forcing the waves to spread out as they run to shore.

The cove was used as one of the filming locations for the much acclaimed 1976 TV film *Nuts In May* starring Roger Solman as Keith Pratt, a man who fully earns his surname, due to his nit-picking obsessions with order and detail. He takes his partner Candice-Marie, played by Alison Steadman, on a holiday under canvas to the beautiful Dorset countryside, escaping the stress of work in London for a week, or at least that was the plan.

This standing stone at the Heritage Centre at Lulworth Cove was unveiled by Prince Charles in 2002.

Cliff erosion has caused the diversion of the coast path above the cove.

The old hand cranked boat winch adds to the rustic charm of the cove.

Records show that the first 'tourists' to visit Lulworth date back to the 16th century. A time when the cottages would have been used as farm workers accommodation, with many, it has been said, supplementing their income from smuggling, an occupation, as we have already discovered was much appreciated by the local gentry and landowners.

The cove, being extremely sheltered, was a famous haunt for smugglers, the unpredictable English Channel weather having little consequence on their activities. One story tells that at daybreak on a summer morning during the early 1700s, several smugglers were approached near the cove running contraband, including brandy. A battle ensued between them and the customs officers, and they were said to have fought like demons when it seemed they were about to lose their precious cargo. The battle was understood to have raged for several hours, attracting many parishioners to the scene, who allegedly subsequently left with some of the abandoned barrels.

A row of coastguard cottages were built in 1824 to house the customs and excise men. At nearby Winfrith, one Charles Weeks had developed a particularly shrewd way of defrauding the revenue, purchasing at auction seized goods then adding them to his smuggled goods for sale at outlets as far afield as London. If challenged he could show receipts detailing that the correct duty had been paid.

Tales of smuggling often conjure up a scene of romance, but as we have already discovered along the coast, the reality was very different, with further evidence found on a tombstone in a Weymouth cemetery with the inscription:

'Sacred to the memory of Lieut. Thos Edward Knight, RN, of Folkestone, Kent, Aged 42, who in the execution of his duty as Chief Officer of the Coastguard was wantonly attacked by a body of smugglers near Lulworth on the night of 28th of June 1832, by whom after being unmercifully beaten he was thrown over the cliff near Durdle Door from the effects of which he died the following day'

The cove was known as Lulwind Cove in Thomas Hardy's *Far From The Madding Crowd*. In September 1920 Thomas Hardy wrote *At Lulworth Cove a Century Back*:

Had I but lived a hundred years ago
I might have gone, as I have gone this year,
By Warmwell Cross on to a Cove I know,
And Time have placed his finger on me there:

"*You see that man?*" – I might have looked, and said,
"O yes: I see him. One that boat has brought
Which dropped down Channel round Saint Alban's Head.
So commonplace a youth calls not my thought."

"*You see that man?*" – "Why yes; I told you; yes:
Of an idling town-sort; thin; hair brown in hue;
And as the evening light scants less and less
He looks up at a star, as many do."

"*You see that man?*" – "Nay, leave me!" then I plead,
"I have fifteen miles to vamp across the lea,
And it grows dark, and I am weary-kneed:
I have said the third time; yes, that man I see!"

"Good. That man goes to Rome – to death, despair;
And no one notes him now but you and I:
A hundred years, and the world will follow him there,
And bend with reverence where his ashes lie."

John Keats had landed at Lulworth Cove a century earlier in September 1820, while a passenger on board the *Maria Crowther* bound for Italy. His last night on English soil was spent at Lulworth Cove and it was here he composed the sonnet *Bright Star, would that I were steadfast as thou art*.

The cove was a famous haunt for smugglers.

113

STAIR HOLE

Stair Hole is another cove in the making, forming to the west of Lulworth Cove.

Stair Hole Cove is forming to the west of Lulworth Cove and it has been suggested that it could become as large as its close neighbour in the far distant future. The forces and land mass that created Lulworth Cove are repeated here, with the sedimentary rocks that were formed underwater having been tilted as the continents collided, now eroded from the continual pounding of the sea. The Portland stone that faces the sea has been breached by waves battering weak points. The small cracks are enlarged into caves that collapse to form arches. The softer Purbeck and Wealden Beds behind have been washed away to create a series of small coves. Stair Hole also featured in the TV film, *Nuts in May*.

The raised Purbeck Beds are made from alternate layers of hard limestone and soft shale. The bands have collapsed into the 'Lulworth Crumple' as the softer shale is unable to withstand the forces of gravity. The effect of cliff erosion on these alternate layers results in the shale being washed away to leave unsupported blocks of Portland stone that will eventually fall onto the beach.

Lulworth Cove and the surrounding pastoral countryside have been recognised as being totally unique and have gained World Heritage status. Lulworth now houses a permanent exhibition located within the Heritage Centre detailing the history and geological importance of the Jurassic Coastline. A standing stone was unveiled by Prince Charles in 2002.

As the sun begins to set, the Island of Portland a dominant feature along this stretch of coast, takes on a silhouette appearance.

WEST LULWORTH

West Lulworth lies less than a mile inland from the sea, another delightful quintessential Dorset village of thatched cobbled stone cottages dating back to the 18th century. The village was once home to a mill up until fire destroyed the building, with just a millpond as evidence today of its existence.

An old Norman Church originally stood in the village centre and was described by John O'Keefe in 1791 as 'very ancient, the smallest I ever saw'. By 1869 the original church had become 'dilapidated' and was demolished. The present church, Holy Trinity, was built of local Purbeck stone with some material used from the original church. The Lychgate was dedicated by the Bishop of Salisbury in 1953 and is built of oak with a tiled roof.

The present church, Holy Trinity, was built in the 19th century of local Purbeck stone, replacing an earlier Norman structure.

The traditional Dorset fingerpost grid reference reveals the location, this one to be in the village of East Lulworth.

EAST LULWORTH

A mile or so east of the cove is East Lulworth, another delightful 'chocolate box' village of cobbled stone and thatched cottages with a traditional village inn. The inn was once the haunt of smugglers, and tradition tells that the landlord, one Richard Champ, worked closely alongside the infamous gang from Osmington Mills. The area was said to be the despair of the customs officers. The Weld Arms dates back to the 17th century, originally built as a row of cottages during the previous century. During World War Two a German Bomber was hit and dropped its cargo of bombs on the village and for half a century one remained embedded in the thatched roof of the pub, discovered by thatchers in 1994.

Lulworth Castle was not built as a fortification, unlike nearby Corfe Castle, but as a hunting lodge during the 17th century, developing as a large country house set at the heart of a large country estate. The castle was originally built by Thomas Howard, 3rd Lord Bindon, to entertain hunting parties. The interior of the castle has seen considerable alteration, keeping up to date with modification over the centuries. The castle interior was devastated by fire in 1929.

Full restoration of the castle was completed by English Heritage in 1998 and the castle and chapel is now open to the public.

Sunlit thatch and threatening skies at East Lulworth.

THE ISLE OF PURBECK

Leaving Lulworth behind, we now enter the diverse and beautiful Isle of Purbeck, not strictly an island but a peninsula surrounded by the English Channel to the south and east and Poole Harbour and the marsh lands of the River Frome on its northern border. The western extent of Purbeck or, to give it the correct title, the Isle of Purbeck, is less defined with most sources referring to Flower's Barrow above Worbarrow Bay as the dividing line. The area is as diverse as you could get anywhere in Britain. Large swathes are now designated Areas of Outstanding Natural Beauty (AONB) with the diversity perhaps no more apparent than the number of species of wild flowers, said to be one of the highest concentration of any comparable area in Britain. This is certainly the part of Dorset to have that wild flower book available as your companion.

Purbeck has, to coin an old phrase, something for everyone, with castles, a heritage railway, oil exploration, delightful olde worlde villages and over 20 miles of awe inspiring varied coast line. Swanage is the main centre of population and culture for Purbeck, with Poole Harbour, one of the worlds largest natural harbours, on its northern edge.

The military also play an active role in the area and it is with that in mind we head for Tyneham, once a quiet Dorset village, just a stones throw from the sea, with a church, a school house and a cluster of cottages. In 1943 all the residents of the village and the surrounding area were driven out so that the Army could train using live ammunition. Years of neglect followed and the village has remained deserted. Thankfully the church and the school house have been restored and are now museums. Access is, though, restricted and you need to check the times. As a rule the walks and the village are open to the public every weekend from 9am Saturday until 7.30pm Sunday, but there are

exceptions, and these are posted well in advance and can be found on the MOD website. The area is also open on bank holidays and during the summer months, but again these need to be confirmed before visiting. The gate to Tyneham is locked each night at dusk and the exhibitions in Tyneham School and Tyneham Church are open from 10am until 4pm.

The area is blessed with delightfully named hamlets and villages.

The church of St Peter in the village of Church Knowle was built during the 13th century.

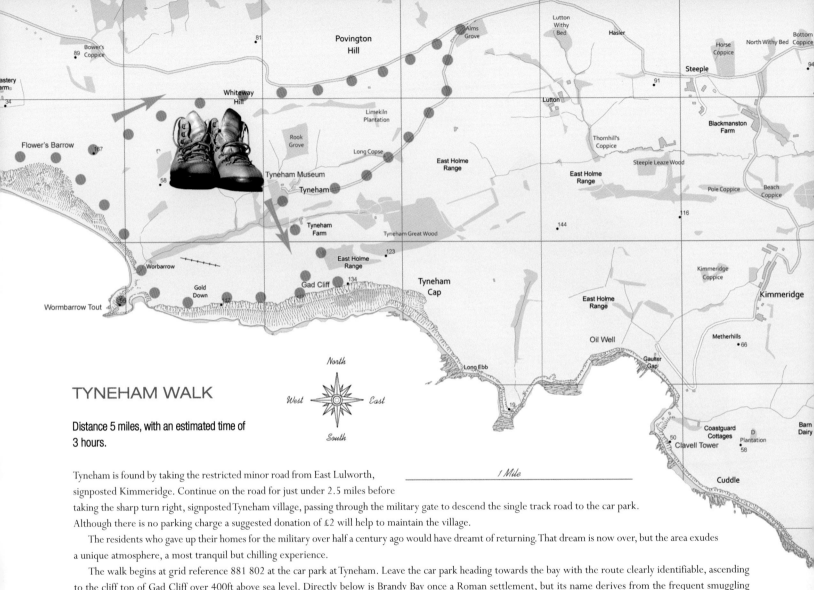

TYNEHAM WALK

Distance 5 miles, with an estimated time of 3 hours.

Tyneham is found by taking the restricted minor road from East Lulworth, signposted Kimmeridge. Continue on the road for just under 2.5 miles before taking the sharp turn right, signposted Tyneham village, passing through the military gate to descend the single track road to the car park. Although there is no parking charge a suggested donation of £2 will help to maintain the village.

The residents who gave up their homes for the military over half a century ago would have dreamt of returning. That dream is now over, but the area exudes a unique atmosphere, a most tranquil but chilling experience.

The walk begins at grid reference 881 802 at the car park at Tyneham. Leave the car park heading towards the bay with the route clearly identifiable, ascending to the cliff top of Gad Cliff over 400ft above sea level. Directly below is Brandy Bay once a Roman settlement, but its name derives from the frequent smuggling activities that would have taken place during the 17th and 18th centuries. Take the cliff path on your right to descend to the promontory of Worbarrow Tout. Great care is needed on this section of the walk as the cliffs are unstable near the edge.

Ordnance Survey data © Crown copyright and database right 2012

Gad Cliff stands over 400ft above sea level. The cliff edges are extremely dangerous and care should be taken at all times. Directly below is Brandy Bay, its name derived from frequent smuggling activities during the 17th and 18th centuries.

The census of 1901 recalls that a remote coastal hamlet of seven cottages and a coastguard station stood here at Worbarrow, with a population of over 50 people, half of them coastguard families. The station was to close in 1911, a decision that saw the population reduced to a level that it never recovered from. Generations of fishermen had lived and worked here with the nearby village of Tyneham providing worship and education for their families.

Worbarrow Bay with the distant cliffs of Arish Mell and Mupe Rocks. Arish Mell beach remains closed to the public due to the threat of live ammunition. In 1959 Arish Mell became the site of a discharge pipe two miles out to sea used by the Atomic Energy Authority on Winfrith Heath. By 1990 plans were drawn up for decommissioning the site.

The coastguard station dated from the early 19th century and the role of the coastguard was not only to save lives but to pursue smugglers and to prevent collection of driftwood. After the station closed William Bond, the owner of the Tyneham estate, had the buildings demolished.

Hill Cottage stood next to the coastguard station and was home to generations of fishing Millers who it was said were active in the smuggling trade, despite living next door to the coastguard. The plaque above the bay tells the story of the hamlet and in particular makes reference to the fishing Millers who it is said had lived in the hamlet for over two centuries. They were descendants of two brothers who had made their way down from Scotland, supposedly Spanish privateers, blown ashore at the time of the Armada in 1588. By 1851 there were 18 Millers living at Worbarrow. By 1943 the remaining residents, who were mostly elderly, were evacuated with Worbarrow becoming part of the Lulworth Ranges.

The plaque details all of the hamlet's dwellings and reveals that only the shell of Gate Cottage remains, clearly visible if taking the path directly back to Tyneham Farm and the car park, avoiding the next part of the walk, the climb to Flower's Barrow.

If completing the full walk the route continues with a rather steep rise over a short distance to the hill fort of Flower's Barrow, standing over 500ft above sea level. The south side of the hill fort is gradually falling into the sea. Minor excavations in 1939, before the army took over, yielded only a limited number of artefacts.

Access is restricted and you need to check the times. As a rule the walks and the village are open to the public every weekend although danger areas remain out of bounds.

Worbarrow Tout.

From the hill fort the walk continues heading east over a grassy path before joining the track that runs alongside the road. Heading all the while easterly where, in a mile and a half from Flower's Barrow, you reach the viewpoint at Povington Hill, where there is a small car park area. The views behind now reveal Worbarrow Tout and distant Portland while east the vast expanse of heathland and distant Poole Harbour, and our first glimpse of the Bournemouth conurbation can be seen. Continue along the road for just under half a mile before taking the sharp right turn, the road back to Tyneham.

The Church of St Mary's at Tyneham was built using limestone rubble and dates from the 13th century. After the villagers left, the church suffered from neglect, with the bells and organ moved to the church at Steeple. Today the church is a museum dedicated to the village, using old photographs and a detailed history, and is seen as a memorial shrine to idyllic village life. A life that was taken away from the population of over 250 who were scattered throughout the entire Parish of Tyneham. The villagers did, however, leave behind what is now a renowned notice pinned to the door of the church.

'Please treat the church and houses with care; we have given up our homes where many of us lived for generations to help win the war to keep men free. We shall return one day and thank you for treating the village kindly.'

The church is now a museum dedicated to the village.

The church has remained as it was when the villagers departed; a note was pinned on the church door requesting that it be treated with care.

The inside of the old village school which has now been restored to its former glory.

The village phone box, ironically, installed not long before evacuation.

'The Copper'. A fire would be light underneath to provide boiling water for washing and steaming.

Known locally as the Row, or Post Office Row, there once stood a bakery, then a general store and the post office where within could be found the only telephone in the village, that was until the addition of the phone box.

The old village school has also been restored to its former glory, although it had closed as early as 1932 when the numbers of pupils fell to around a dozen. The inside and outside now reflects what life would have been like in a village school during the early 1900s.

A distinctive feature of the church at Steeple is the lack of a steeple.

KIMMERIDGE

Leaving behind the lost village the journey continues within sight of the sea, at first heading through the hamlet of Steeple where the ancient church is well worth a visit. The first thing that is noticeable is that the church lacks a steeple. A stone coat of arms engraved in the porch is identical to that of George Washington's, showing stars and stripes and is depicted on the barrel-vaulted roof panels. The flag of the US capital hangs inside the church, the association dating back to 1390 when the stars and stripes heraldically joined the crusader cross of the Lawrence family, at the time when Edmund Lawrence married Agnes de Wessington.

There is no sandy beach at Kimmeridge, the bedrock visible under the waves extending out to sea, known as the Kimmeridge Ledges.

The quiet country lane continues toward the sea arriving at Kimmeridge, where thatched and slate roofed cottages make up the tiny village, less than a mile from the sheltered bay that it takes its name from. A toll road leads to the coast where low cliffs of black shale ring the bay. There is no sandy beach at Kimmeridge instead it is littered with rocks that yield a plentiful supply of fossil ammonites. The bedrock is visible under the waves extending out to sea below the cliffs and is known as the Kimmeridge Ledges. The rocks can be explored at times of very low tide.

Above the bay British Petroleum's 'nodding donkey' has been producing oil since 1959. The cliffs were first exploited for oil shale as far back as the Iron Age and during the Roman occupation, with the latter day explorations beginning during the 1930s. The site may be small but the beam pump, or nodding donkey, produces around 65 barrels a day, although in the early years production had reached over 300 barrels a day. Known as Kimmeridge KI the site is now the oldest working oil pump in the UK. The oil is transported to Wytch Farm by tanker then piped to storage tanks on Southampton Water before shipping to a refinery.

Set high above the Kimmeridge Ledges on the cliff top is Clavell Tower, originally built in 1830 as a folly and observatory by the Revd John Richards Clavell of Smedmore. The folly was built over four storeys with a very distinctive colonnade. Thomas Hardy is said to have brought Eliza Nicholls, his first love, on many visits. During the 19th and early 20th century the tower was used by coastguards before suffering dereliction, its structure further damaged by fire in the 1930s. You would be forgiven if you had visited the area many years ago and are now returning, thinking something seems different, and you would be right. In 2007 the tower was dismantled brick by brick with the 16,000 bricks painstakingly numbered and moved over 80ft inland, away from the eroding cliff edge.

Kimmeridge and Clavell Tower bathed in early morning light.

The distinctive silhouette of Clavell Tower. The tower was originally built in 1830 as a folly and observatory by the Reverend John Richards Clavell of Smedmore.

Following its capture by Cromwell he ensured Corfe Castle could never be used against him again by blowing it up in 1646.

CORFE CASTLE

The chalk ridge of the Purbeck Hills extend from west of Dorchester to Old Harry Rocks, and would have once continued to the Isle of Wight. To the north the valley of the River Frome divides the hills and the Dorset heath lands. At Corfe Castle the hills are broken in two sections leaving a steep rounded hill between the ridge, its prominent position the perfect location for a stronghold, protecting the principle route through the hills. Today the road from Wareham to Swanage passes through this narrow gap and is dominated by the ruins of the mediaeval Corfe Castle, from which the village takes its name.

During the invasion of William the Conqueror in 1066, orders went out to enlarge the castle to defend the road leading from Swanage, with an original wooden castle rebuilt of stone, with further additions added during the 13th century. The castle was sold by Elizabeth I in 1572. During the Civil War in 1643 the castle withstood a siege by Parliamentarians while in the ownership of the royalist Sir John Bankes. Following his death in 1644 further attempts were made to destroy the castle. Tradition has it that due to treachery from within, the castle finally fell to the Parliamentarians in 1646. Following its capture Cromwell ensured it could never be used against him again by blowing it up. A testament to its great strength lies in the fact that the castle remains today much as it did after the destruction in 1646.

The castle is owned by the National Trust with admission charged. Once within the castle walls, the true extent of the magnificent fortified location soon becomes apparent, although perhaps its strategic importance can be best appreciated from the various vantage points around the village. The castle is inhabited, not by humans, but Soay sheep used by the National Trust to ensure the grass is well mown. This ancient breed originates from the islands of the St Kilda archipelago, a group of islands some 41 miles west of the Outer Hebrides, and are believed to be the oldest breed of domestic sheep, although how they got there no one really knows.

Ravens now roost once again at the castle, and as beholds the Tower of London many believed that a terrible tragedy would befall the castle should they leave. Legend tells us this is what came about way back in 1638.

The village is dominated by the ruins of the mediaeval Corfe Castle from which it takes its name.

There is, however, a great deal more to Corfe Castle than just the castle, although it is the dominating reason to visit. A model village has faithfully reproduced a replica of how the castle looked before being blown up by the Parliamentarians. Opened in 1966 and built to a 1/20th scale, the model village depicts the castle and village as it was in 1646.

A most unusual feature of the village, built mainly during the 18th century is that most of its picturesque grey limestone cottages have delightful undulating stone roofs, a fact not gone unnoticed with many historical TV and feature films, using the village as a setting. Tradition has it that much of the building material for the cottages no doubt came from the ruins of the castle.

The preserved Swanage Railway has a station here at Corfe Castle, the buildings as would be expected built of local stone. When the line closed in 1972 the station buildings were purchased by Dorset County Council who in 1992 granted the Swanage Railway a licence to restore the buildings, the re-laid track having reached as far as Corfe Castle from Swanage the previous year. Corfe Castle station has now been restored to as near the original condition as possible.

ENID BLYTON

Enid Blyton first came to Dorset in 1931 and much of the countryside, castles and islands described in her stories were inspired by the years she spent visiting Swanage and the Isle of Purbeck. It has even been said that the origins of PC Plod in *Noddy* was inspired by the local Studland Police Constable.

The *Famous Five* stories revolve around the children, Julian, Dick, and Anne. They have an uncle Quentin in the country where they are destined to spend their summer holidays because the usual family holiday hotel is booked up. Their uncle, a scientist, has a daughter Georgina, a tomboy who prefers to be called, or insists on being called George, and of course their faithful dog Timmy.

George, having spent most of her life left to her own devices, is initially suspicious of the newcomers, but in time they all become the best of friends, and share many adventures. The adventures begin with the children arriving for their holiday on the train at what may well have been Corfe Station. The *Famous Five* books ran to 21 adventures written between 1942 and 1963 and to this day have never gone out of print. Enid died at the age of 71 on 28 November 1968.

Leaving behind Corfe Castle and for a short time the railway, the journey continues heading back through the gap in the chalk hills, following the A351 for a short distance, before taking the minor road bearing right signposted Worth Matravers.

The preserved Swanage Railway has a delightful station situated here at Corfe Castle.

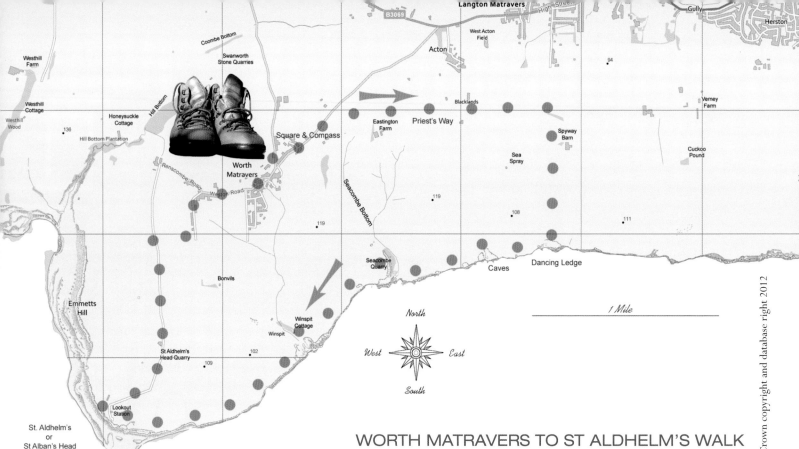

Ordnance Survey data © Crown copyright and database right 2012

WORTH MATRAVERS TO ST ALDHELM'S WALK

Distance 7 miles, with an estimated time of 3.5–4 hours.

The steep streets and stone cottages that adorn the village of Worth Matravers are the starting point for a walk that includes some of the most dramatic coastline Dorset has to offer. The route takes in St Aldhelm's or St Alban's Head. Initially following the Priests Way from Worth Matravers for part of the outward route toward Swanage, passing several stone quarries before following the delightfully undulating coast path, taking in St Aldhelm's Head on the return journey. Parking is available in Worth Matravers at grid reference 974 776.

From the car park turn right, down the hill turning immediately left at the junction passing the village pub, the Square and Compass, taking its name from the tools used by local quarrymen to cut the stone. Within the pub is a fossil museum covering over 60 years of collecting, with fossil finds from Purbeck and several archaeological finds on display, these dating from Mesolithic and Neolithic times through to Bronze Age and the Roman invasion. The museum and, of course, the pub is well worth a visit, a good option to take at the end of the walk. Take the road that leads out of the village, crossing a stile on your right taking the footpath to emerge at Eastington farm. You now join the Priests Way. Continue for a mile and a quarter of easy walking passing stone quarries to take a right turn where the track intersects with the track from Langton Matravers, the track leading you to Dancing Ledge, passing Spyway Barn on the way.

The flat topped 'Dancing Ledge' was used as a customary landing point for contraband before the onward journey to Langton Matravers.

The Grade II listed building dates from the early 19th century and is constructed from traditional rubble stone with a stone and slate roof, characteristic of this area of Dorset. The barn was purchased by the National Trust in the early 1990s; the barn houses a display room highlighting local wildlife, conservation and history of the area.

Spyway refers to smuggling activities that took place along the coast with the flat topped 'Dancing Ledge' used as a customary landing point. Contraband was then taken up over the cliffs to be stored at Spyway, before the onward journey to Langton Matravers, where tradition tells that kegs were stored in a void above the ceiling in the church roof. Continue past the barn where the next field yields a surprise, a sculpture of a Limousin cow, important for grazing the grassland.

The fields are now managed as traditional hay meadows with no fertilizer or chemical usage, ensuring they remain a haven for wildlife. During spring and summer the cliffs are alive with a plethora of wild flowers including cowslips, chalk milkwort and rare orchids. The cliffs above Dancing Ledge are relatively low compared to other sections of the Dorset coast no doubt a major encouragement for the smugglers.

Leaving behind Dancing Ledge, the walk and the outstanding coastal views continue, turning right to follow the South West Coast Path to Seacombe. A short distance inland from the Dancing Ledge is an area of grazing land known locally as 'Scratch Arse Ware' the 'Ware' derived from rough grazing, as to the first part, who knows! Continue along the short tufted grass providing delightful walking, to reach the well hidden cove of Seacombe Cliff. The cliffs around the cove were an important source of Portland limestone, with widespread mine passages along the edges of the cliff evidently visible. The seabed here is made up of a wave cut platform.

Ledges and caves are abundant on this stretch of coast. In the far distance is Anvil Point, Swanage.

High above the sea at the site of an old quarry that closed in the 19th century is a precarious stone monolith, made up of two different types of stone, said to have been left to aid safe passage through the St Alban's Race. A sea ledge extends some five miles out to sea off St Alban's Head, the height of the ledge forcing the fast moving tides to the surface, creating the turbulent waters of the race.

The vaulted stone building of St Aldhelm's Chapel dates from at least the 13th century.

At Seacombe the path heads slightly inland before turning left, passing through a gate to begin the ascent to Winspit, another popular landing stage for smuggling until an unfortunate incident resulted in a coastguard being placed on permanent duty. The path descends to the old quarries at Winspit leaving no doubt as to the importance of this area for Portland stone, the quarrying activity ceasing in the 1940s. Many of the caves are now closed to help the conservation of bats. The quarry may seem familiar to the first generation of *Dr Who* fans, as it was used as a location in the series *Underwater Menace* first broadcast in 1967 and then as planet Skargo in the serial *Destiny of the Daleks* in 1979. Winspit has some of Britain's best preserved Strip Lynchets. These mediaeval strips of land show how important the role of agriculture would have once been to the area.

Evidence of past quarrying activity can be seen on the cliffs.

Continue west ascending to West Man. Close to the head is a memorial to the early development of radar carried out near this point. The plaque is inscribed:

'This memorial commemorates the radar research carried out at Worth Matravers from 1940–1942 which was crucial to the winning of the war and the birth of modern telecommunications. The stainless steel memorial represents not only two radar dishes but also a large fire basket, reflecting both modern and ancient methods to warn of the threat of invasion.'

ST ALDHELM'S HEAD or ST ALBAN'S HEAD as detailed on OS mapping, is a limestone headland with a row of former coastguard cottages and a coastguard lookout, now used by the National Coastwatch Institution. The headland is also home to St Aldhelm's Chapel, dedicated to the Bishop of Sherbourne, the vaulted stone building dating from at least the 13th century. A local legend tells that, in the 12th century, a bride and groom were sailing around the headland watched by the bride's father. They were drowned when a storm suddenly arose and capsized the boat. The father was said to have built the chapel in their memory and a light was always to be kept burning to warn other sailors. In 2005 a new altar table was consecrated by the Archbishop of Canterbury, appropriately made from local Portland stone.

Mariners refer to the head as St Alban's named after a martyr from the third century. By the 18th century the chapel had fallen into disrepair but was restored and re-opened in 1874.

This memorial commemorates the radar research carried out at Worth Matravers from 1940–42.

The Square and Compass dates back to 1776 when it first became an ale house.

From the head a rough track runs for a mile and a half, passing on the way a stone quarry before bearing right to go past a barn. The track emerges on to Weston Road. Turn right to follow the lane back to the centre of the village. A well deserved rest and refreshment can be taken at the tea rooms or the Square and Compass, where a look at the fossil and local finds museum awaits.

SQUARE AND COMPASS FOSSIL MUSEUM

The Square and Compass dates back to 1776 when it became an ale house, previously a pair of cottages set on a bluff overlooking the village and the sea. Known at that time as the Sloop, it had connections with the smuggling trade and many skirmishes were said to have taken place with the excise men on St Aldhelm's Head. The name changed during the 1830s with a new tenant landlord Charles Bower, who by trade was a stone mason. In 1907 the pub was taken over by the Newman's. The years between the wars saw the pub become fashionable among the creative set with the visitors book signed by actors Leslie Banks and Gwen Franco-Davis and the artist Augustus John and cartoonist Low to name but a few. The Square has retained its character.

The Museum at the Square & Compass has its origins dating back 60 years to when Ray Newman was the landlord. His son Charlie became fascinated with his father's collection and set up the museum as a tribute to him.

On show in the museum, primarily from Purbeck, is a fascinating collection of specimens discovered in the Kimmeridge clay, Portland and Purbeck stone. Specimens from Lyme Regis, North Somerset and Whitby can also be seen alongside the local finds. During the 1960s Ray Newman's collection of fossils from the Wealden Beds and Swanage was identified and catalogued by the Natural History Museum. Archaeological finds are also on display and include Mesolithic and Neolithic flint tools. Items from both the Bronze Age and Roman occupation are on display including potsherds, coins and axe fragments. A collection of clay pipes are on display from an era when the landlord would sell a clay pipe filled with tobacco, ready to smoke!

Previously a pair of cottages, the Square and Compass is set on a bluff overlooking the village and the sea.

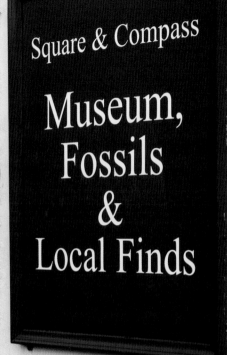

The Museum at the Square and Compass has its origins dating back over 60 years.

Shipwrecks during the 18th century were a common occurrence and on display are artefacts found from the wreck of the *Halswell*, which went down off Seacombe Cliffs in 1786. The *Halswell*, outward bound for India, encountered severe storms in the channel and was driven onto a lee shore. Despite the heroic efforts of the captain and his crew to manoeuvre the ship to safety, she hit the rocks below Seacombe Cliff. Over a hundred souls perished as she went down, including the captain. History tells that 70 passengers were rescued from the cliffs but a further 60 who had made it that far died from the cold or drowning. The magnitude of the disaster was such a tragic loss that it moved King George III to pay a visit to Seacombe Cliffs.

The coin collection includes a George III cartwheel penny. In 1797 King George III struck a 1d and a 2d coin that was so large they became known as the 'cartwheel'. The coin featured King George's portrait on the obverse and the seated figure of Britannia on the reverse.

Some of the buckles on display date from the 15th century.

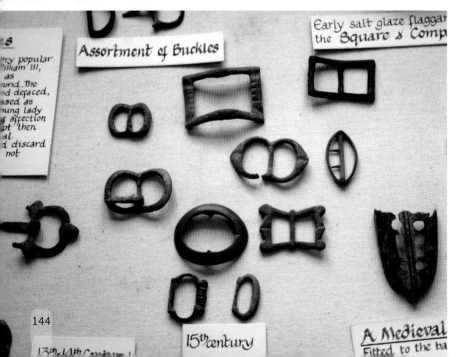

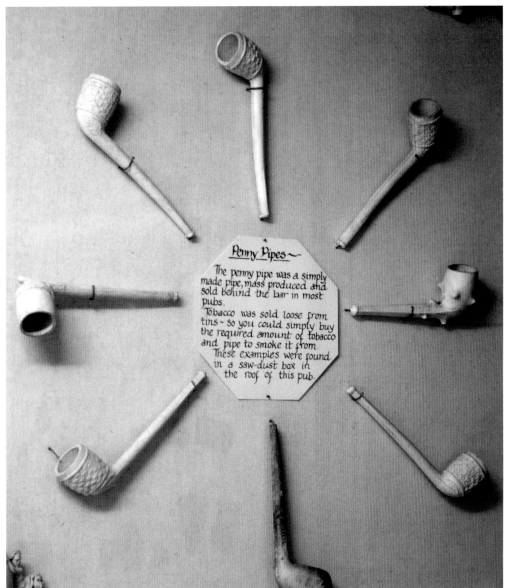

Penny Pipes ~

The penny pipe was a simply made pipe, mass produced and sold behind the bar in most pubs.
Tobacco was sold loose from tins ~ so you could simply buy the required amount of tobacco and pipe to smoke it from.
These examples were found in a saw-dust box in the roof of this pub.

Early 19th century Powder Flask

An early 19th-century powder flask.

Penny Pipes; the penny pipe was a simply made pipe mass produced and sold behind the bar in most pubs. Tobacco was sold loose so you could simply buy the required amount and a pipe to smoke it from.

During the 1960s Ray Newman's collection of fossils from the Wealden Beds and Swanage was identified and catalogued by the Natural History Museum.

The duck pond is delightfully situated in the centre of the village in the midst of traditional stone roofed cottages.

The church of St Nicholas of Myra at Worth Matravers.

The church of St Nicholas of Myra is one of the oldest in Dorset, dating from Saxon times. Most of the building is of a rubble stone, strengthened during the 12th century by the Normans who added buttresses, and a new roof. The church underwent complete restoration during the 19th century.

In 1774 Benjamin Jesty, a farmer from Yetminster, infected his family deliberately with cowpox, in a successful attempt to protect them from an outbreak of smallpox. This was the first use of a cowpox vaccination ever recorded, some 20 years before Edward Jenner was given a reward of £10,000 from the House of Commons, for discovering and promoting the vaccination. Benjamin Jesty died in Worth Matravers on 16 April 1816 and was buried in a prominent position in the parish churchyard where his widow Elizabeth would also be buried alongside in 1824. Both headstones are Listed, first and foremost due to their historic interest. The full inscription on Jesty's headstone reads:

> '(Sacred) To the Memory of Benj:m Jesty (of Downshay) who departed this Life, April 16th 1816 aged 79 Years. He was born at Yetminster in this County, and was an upright honest Man: particularly noted for having been the first Person (known) that Introduced the Cow Pox by Inoculation, and who from his great strength of mind made the Experiment from the (Cow) on his Wife and two Sons in the Year 1774.'

As we leave behind the historic Worth Matravers, the traditional seaside town of Swanage now awaits a mere 3 miles east.

SWANAGE

The seaside town of Swanage sits between towering downs that end as cliff rimmed promontories overlooking a sandy bay, with the old streets weaving their way down to the sea front. Originally a small fishing village and port, it was also an important quarrying centre during the Roman occupation. Mentioned in the *Domesday Book* as Sonwic and known as Sandwich in the 17th century when it was still a small village, the name Swanage evolved during the 18th century.

It would, however, be the next century that would see the town flourish with the coming of the railways during the Victorian era. The station opened in 1885 by the London and South Western Railway Company. With transport links improving and journey time diminishing, the resort became popular with the wealthy classes. It was renowned for its fine sea air, good weather and direct access from London. The line from Wareham survived 87 years but finally fell as a result of the Beeching axe, although it survived longer than some, closing in 1972, with the track bed fully lifted despite fierce local opposition.

The increase in popularity of the resort led to the building of a new pier, opened in 1897 to accommodate pleasure steamers from Poole and Bournemouth. Regular services continued for over half a century with the last departing in 1966. The pier was allowed to fall into disrepair, with attempts to renovate during the 1980s failing, its saviour being the Swanage Pier Trust set up in 1993. The trust raised over a million pounds to restore the pier with a ferry service now running to Poole and the paddle steamers *Waverley* and MV *Balmoral* annual summer visitors.

The traditional British seaside holiday is alive and well, particularly here at Swanage, with its sheltered bay and sandy beach, ideal for the family complete with amusement arcades, Punch and Judy, and traditionally striped deck chairs.

Opposite left: George Burt brought back many items from London as ballast for his sailing ketches on their return after transporting Purbeck stone to the capital during the 19th century. Structures, bollards and street furniture that were discarded during the rapid redevelopment of London provided necessary ballast for the return journey, earning Swanage the title of 'Little London by the Sea'. The bollards lining the quayside bear evidence to this. A town trail is available at Swanage Museum and Heritage Centre in The Square.

Opposite right: A pebble mosaic based on the Swanage emblem of three fish in a roundel enhances The Square.

The jetty provides a good opportunity to rest and soak up the atmosphere.

149

The original Swanage Pier was constructed in the mid 19th century for the Swanage Pier and Tramway Company. The pier was built to ship stone with the intention to link the quarries at Langton Matravers by horse drawn carts using a rail track. The ambitious plan never reached fruition, although remnants of the old track can still be seen today along the quayside. A new longer pier was built at the end of the 19th century to cater for the increasing number of visitors by steamer from Bournemouth.

One of the most characteristic images of the seaside has to be that of the deck chair. The deck chair featured on many of the early ocean liner brochures and railway posters, tempting holiday makers to the seaside, to enjoy the summer sun. The first 'folding chair' was patented in 1886 for use aboard ships during the golden age of cruise liners, with the chairs becoming known as deck chairs, very practical as, when not being used for relaxation by the passengers, they could be neatly folded and stacked away for storage. The popularity of the chair would see them appearing on promenades and beaches throughout Britain, a sight that can still be seen today, a testament to the original chair designed by John Thomas Moore, although a variation is said to have existed as far back as the ancient Egyptians.

ROYAL NATIONAL LIFEBOAT INSTITUTION (RNLI)

Stories of shipwrecks during the 18th and early 19th centuries abound the length of the Dorset coast as we have discovered with tragic tales at Chesil Beach, Weymouth and Worth Matravers. Modern day navigation aids now assist the mariner but one service they are most dependant on is the Royal National Lifeboat Institution (RNLI). The institution was founded as a charity in 1824, later to be renamed the RNLI in 1854.

Sir William Hillary is credited with founding the National Institution, for the preservation of life from shipwreck. From his home on the Isle of Man, he saw firsthand the tragic loss of life from dozens of shipwrecks, becoming involved in many rescue attempts. Sir William appealed to the Navy and the government for help in forming a national institute for the preservation of lives and property from shipwreck and, with the support of London MP Thomas Wilson and the West Indian Merchants Chairman George Hibbert, the institution was formed.

Gulls are one of the most characteristic images of the seaside.

Timber groynes were first constructed on the beach at Swanage in 1925. Eighteen new timber groynes were put in place in 2005, the same year seeing 90,000 cubic metres of sand deposited on the beach. The work that was finally completed in June 2006 was necessary to hold the sand in place.

Robert Charles Brown is an all weather Mersey Class lifeboat with a range of 140 miles and has been on station since 1992.

During the early 19th century, it was estimated that 1,800 ships were wrecked around the coasts of Britain every year. Coastal communities would watch helplessly as ships became stranded and broke up. Records do show that in 1730 there was a rescue boat in Liverpool, and in 1785 in Bamburgh, Northumberland, the first purpose-built life boat was patented by Lionel Lukin. Within 20 years, upward of 30 boats had been built and they were saving lives around the coast of Britain.

Rowing boats were initially used by the institution with the introduction of sailing boats during the 1850s. Six steam powered craft were added to the fleet during the 1890s before their development was abandoned in favour of petrol, during the early 1900s. The first motor driven lifeboat was introduced as early as 1905, but could prove unreliable so sail rigging was still required.

The iconic inflatable was introduced in 1963 to deal with rescues inshore. 1972 saw the first B Class rigid inflatable boats, with today's B and D class lifeboats being direct descendants, now making up the bulk of the RNLI fleet.

Larger all-weather lifeboats were being developed, with each new incarnation faster and safer than its predecessor. There are now five classes of all-weather lifeboat in the RNLI fleet, with a variety of sizes, draughts and launch and recovery methods, suitable for all areas of the British and Irish coastlines.

For the RNLI's first 100 years, lifeboats were mostly launched and recovered from their local beaches. Hauling the lifeboat during launch and recovery was done by women, as most of the men were onboard and often farmers loaned their horses to help bear the weight.

Most large, all-weather lifeboats are designed to be launched from a slipway, or to lie afloat. Beach launches are still common, particularly with the smaller, inshore lifeboats with specially adapted tractors to do the hauling.

The lifeboat station here in Swanage at Peveril Point is one of the busiest in the UK, and one of only three stations manned with a slipway launched 'Mersey Class' lifeboat and a D class inflatable, to deal with rescues close to shore.

The new Mersey Class lifeboat has been on station since 1992 and was named *Robert Charles Brown* after the much respected lifeboat man who served for over 50 years, and was awarded the BEM for his service. *Robert Charles Brown* is an all weather lifeboat with a range of 140 miles and accommodates a crew of six.

The Wellington Clock Tower was originally built as a memorial to the Duke of Wellington, however, the clock kept poor time and a statue of the Duke proved too expensive. By 1860, it was obstructing traffic around London Bridge so George Burt brought it back to Swanage as ballast on one of his boats and rebuilt it, overlooking the pier.

The NCI station at Peveril Point is located at Lat: 50 36.43N Long: 001 56.93W.

NCI Watchkeepers provide the eyes and ears along the coast, monitoring radio channels providing a listening watch in times of poor visibility.

THE NATIONAL COASTWATCH INSTITUTION

The National Coastwatch Institution (NCI) is an entirely voluntary organisation keeping a visual watch along the UK shores. Each of the 46 stations strategically positioned throughout the UK as here at Peveril Point assists in the protection and preservation of life at sea around the coastline of the UK.

While technology and sophisticated systems are aids to improved safety, a computer cannot spot a distress flare, an overturned boat or yachtsman or fishermen in trouble. NCI watchkeepers provide the eyes and ears along the coast, monitoring radio channels providing a listening watch in times of poor visibility. The staff are fully trained to deal with emergencies, offering a variety of skills and expertise.

Peveril Point is one of the most dangerous areas for shipping on the Dorset coast. A combination of strong tides and underwater rock ledges have caused the wreck of many ships, and loss of life. One such incident is said to have occurred in AD 877 when King Alfred was said to have lured a fleet of Viking long boats, who were occupying Wareham, out around Peveril Point, the treacherous waters claiming the entire fleet.

The Peveril Ledge reaches far out into Swanage Bay. Beneath the water the limestone ledges create a turbulent sea. With little depth of water the ledges have claimed many wrecks, the safe passage beyond the distant red marker buoy. The old coastguard station overlooks this most treacherous area of water, now manned by volunteers from the National Coastwatch Institution. In the distance the Isle of Wight can be seen.

House-leek clings to the cliffs above Peveril Point, flowering June to September.

Back on the promenade an opportunity presents itself to view the panorama of Swanage Bay.

The Great Globe, one of the largest stone spheres in the world, is constructed of Portland stone and weighs a colossal 40 tonnes with a diameter of 10ft.

South of the town is Durlston Park, a relatively young addition in the grand scheme of historical buildings and parks. During the mid 1800s the area was owned and farmed by several families before a large share was purchased by George Burt in 1863, a local stone mason who had moved to London to work with his uncle, John Mowlem. It was Burt's ambitious plan with the help from his uncle's wealth to transform the village into a major seaside town.

George Burt retired in 1886 and set about acquiring more land and building Durlston Head Castle. Never a castle in the manner of Edward I castle building, more a folly built as a restaurant for the estate. The Victorian age was a period of great advancement and culture and the estate is the home to his Great Globe, one of the largest stone spheres in the world. Constructed of Portland stone, it weighs a colossal 40 tonnes with a diameter of 10ft. The globe was constructed in Greenwich and transported to Swanage by boat. The globe comprises 15 segments, dowelled together with the carved surface detailing the continents and oceans as known in the 1880s.

George Burt carried out significant landscaping of the estate, introducing a variety of plants from around the world. The park has been in the ownership and care of Dorset County Council for over 35 years with the 280 acres of countryside home to a vast diversity of wildlife that includes over 500 species of plant, 250 species of bird and over 30 different species of butterfly.

A lighthouse was established at Anvil Point in Swanage in 1881, a short distance west of Durlston Head. Built form local stone, the tower is only 39ft high with the light set 147ft above Mean High Water. The light was positioned at this point to provide vessels with a clear line from Portland while to the east it guides vessels away from the Christchurch Ledge leading them safely into the Solent. The light was originally illuminated by a paraffin vapour burner, then oil before conversion to electricity in the 1960s. The lighthouse became fully automated in 1991. The characteristic of the lighthouse is a white flash every 10 seconds, although the light is now somewhat dimmer than it used to be. Its range has been reduced from 24 nautical miles to just 9 nautical miles by Trinity House, following a review of all its 600 lights in 2010.

Often the question is asked of the disparity between a statute mile and a nautical mile. The reasoning being a mile on land is measured as 1,760yd, whereas a nautical mile, used for all air and sea travel is 2,026yd, the calculation taking account of the curvature of the earth.

When George Burt retired in 1886, he turned his attention to developing his estate and the building of Durlston Head Castle. Three granite pillars, originally designed for Trafalgar Square, were placed at the entrance to the Castle each individually inscribed with the words Durlston, Head and Castle.

Swanage Cottage Hospital was built in the early 1890s by the children of George Burt, as a tribute to their father. Like his uncle before him George salvaged stones, tiles and at times complete structures from London, bringing them back to Swanage, often referred to as 'little London'. The mosaic over the door almost certainly came from London and could have been part of the consignment of tiles salvaged from the House of Parliament, which the firm renovated. The origins of the cottage hospital can be traced back to the early 19th century to provide care for local people, avoiding long journeys to county hospitals.

The interior still retains some of the original features including a fireplace, complete with fire buckets, and a stained-glass panel now rehoused, taken from the entrance door where it once held pride of place.

Across Swanage Bay, our final destination, Bournemouth, can be seen shimmering on the horizon. As the road climbs north crossing Ballard Down, the coastal settlement of Studland and the vast expanse of heathland will come into view, but not before a delightful nostalgic journey recreating the halcyon days of steam, on the magnificently restored Swanage Railway.

The interior still retains some of the original features including a fireplace, a stained-glass panel and the exterior mosaic cottage hospital name above the entrance.

SWANAGE RAILWAY

The railway first came to Swanage in 1885 and was operated by the London & South Western Railway Company. Between 1847 and 1877 several attempts had been made to get a bill through parliament for a railway from the existing line at Wareham, to Swanage. All these attempts were thwarted by the residents of Wareham who objected to the line going through the centre of the town. In 1880 the local businessman and magistrate, George Burt, succeeded in getting a bill before parliament for a Swanage branch, avoiding the centre of Wareham. Construction of the line commenced on 5 May 1883 and the first public train left Swanage station on 20 May 1885.

Rebuilt Bulleid Pacific No. 34028 Eddystone stands at Harman's Cross.

The signal box at Corfe Castle.

Ex LSWR 0–4–4 tank M7 No.53 was built in 1905 and was based at Bournemouth for a short time during 1964 working the Swanage branch line before being withdrawn from regular service the same year. Class M7 No.53 was renumbered during the British Rail era to M7 30053. In 2009 the M7 was repainted in wartime Southern Railway black livery and renumbered 53.

The first proposal of closure came in August 1966 but failed, with the next attempt by British Rail being in October 1967. That proposal also failed because the required Transport Users' Consultative Committee hearing required by the 1962 Transport Act, backed the objections of residents and councils. British Rail (BR) unsuccessfully tried to close the line in October 1969, and yet again in January 1970, with residents and councils again objecting to replacement bus services. They did not believe BR's claims that the Swanage branch lost £79,000 during 1968. Further closure deadlines of May and September 1970 also came and went. The new BR timetable for 1971 did not encourage people to use the trains when it warned that the service between Wareham and Swanage could be withdrawn. In November 1971 another closure date was given by BR – Monday 3 January 1972. This time, there would be no more deferment and no reprieve.

In January 1972 British Rail closed the line and lifted the track.

For the next three years Swanage Railway Society members fought to persuade the local councils that had bought the disused trackbed to lease them the land, so track relaying work could start. The councils took a lot of persuading because the job seemed too immense; how could a group of people rebuild a whole branch line? Finally, by the summer of 1975, and following a referendum among the people of Swanage, the councils agreed to lease the trackbed to the fledgling Swanage Railway. Now, the promises had to be fulfilled and the dream had to be made a reality.

More than 30 years of work began at Swanage station starting in February 1976, when the volunteers gained access to the boarded up and disused buildings. During the spring of 1977 permission was given for the first track to be laid. Over the years everything needed to rebuild and run the railway had to be brought in by road transporter.

Steadily, the buildings were restored and the tracks re-laid at Swanage using a hand crane. In August 1979 the first public 'push-pull' trains ran the few hundred yards from a temporary scaffolding platform under the Northbrook Road Bridge, to behind the engine shed, with the ticket price 10 pence. The motive power was a small industrial diesel shunter and the stock was a half-painted Bulleid carriage. By Easter 1980 the track had been re-laid back into the main platform at Swanage and the new operating season saw the first steam locomotive brought into service, a small oil burning industrial saddle tank, named *Richard Trevithick*.

Trains continued to run the few hundred yards from Swanage station until Easter 1984. Operations were then extended to the one mile mark at Herston, on the outskirts of the town, where a halt with a run-round loop was built and consequently the trains no longer needed to operate as 'push-pull'. In 1986, a major obstacle to the extension of the railway was eliminated when the county council voted that Corfe Castle station should again be used as a railway and not demolished for a bypass. Trackbed clearing and track-laying work continued and in July 1987 trains started running to the one and a half mile point near New Barn.

During 1988, Dorset's first new station in more than 50 years, was built at Harman's Cross, three miles from Swanage. With the increased length of line, most of it at a climb of up to 1 in 76, ex-industrial saddle tank steam locomotives were dispensed with, and ex-BR varieties were hired in. The first public trains ran up to Harman's Cross in March 1989, after the station was officially opened by BR Southern Region general manager Gordon Pettitt.

Trackbed clearing and track-laying work continued and Corfe Castle was at last reached in the summer of 1991. In the same year everything that had been achieved on the Swanage Railway since 1975 came within a hair's breadth of being eliminated because of a serious financial crisis, one that almost led to bankruptcy. Licking their wounds, picking themselves up and dusting themselves down, the railway volunteers began to start work to eradicate a debt of almost £500,000, a job that would take several years. Track-laying work resumed and the site of Norden Station and its park and ride car park was reached in April 1992.

The first passenger train ran to Corfe Castle and Norden on Saturday 12 August, 1995. On the Wareham end was M7 No. 30053 while on the Swanage end was unrebuilt Battle of Britain class Bulleid Pacific No. 34072 *257 Squadron*.

With the increase in operations and train frequencies, the first signal box was opened at Harman's Cross in July 1997. Swanage followed in March 2003, and Corfe Castle's signal box was reopened in February 2005, with trains passing at the station for the first time since the last BR train of 1 January 1972. A tribute to everyone involved in their creation and restoration, all three signal boxes having won coveted national awards.

Meanwhile, the summer of 1999 saw the start of the final track laying push from Norden to the boundary with the national railway system at Motala.

On 3 January 2002, exactly 30 years to the day since BR closed the Swanage branch, the Swanage Railway's tracks met the Network Rail stopblock and a symbolic golden chair screw was sunk into the final sleeper to mark the historic occasion. Thanks to the help of Network Rail and Virgin Trains, a temporary weekend connection was installed in September 2002, so that a new Virgin Voyager diesel train could run down to Swanage. The diesel was officially named *Dorset Voyager* by two long-time Swanage Railway volunteers. Negotiations continued with Network Rail and in the summer of 2006, a permanent connection was installed and approved at Motala, the historic stopblock being craned out for the last time.

It was on Thursday 10 May 2007 that the permanent connection was used for the first time. Not since the track lifting trains of 1972 had a train run from Wareham to Swanage via a permanent connection.

The fireman aboard the engine has to keep the fire hot, steam pressure up, and water in the boiler.

REBUILT WEST COUNTRY
34028 *EDDYSTONE*

Entering service in April 1946 No 21C128 *Eddystone* took up regular duties on the Kent coast service to London Victoria. Nationalisation of the railways in 1948 saw *Eddystone* renumbered as 34028 and reallocated to Exmouth Junction, heading up the Atlantic Coast Express and the Devon Belle.

Eddystone was one of the first Bulleid light Pacific's to be rebuilt in 1958 and was then transferred to Bournemouth, initially working the Weymouth to Waterloo main line.

Eddystone became a regular on the Somerset and Dorset route between Bournemouth and Bath and was often photographed on the most famous of the S&D trains, The Pines Express. The Somerset and Dorset was never a high speed line as it had to negotiate the Mendip Hills in Somerset, necessitating an arduous climb to over 800ft above sea level at Masbury summit, no doubt contributing to its often used affectionate title the 'Slow and Dirty'.

May 1964 was the end of the line for *Eddystone*, being withdrawn from service, ending up inevitably at the Barry scrapyard in South Wales.

Eddystone was saved by the Southern Pacific Rescue Group, arriving at Selling from the Barry scrapyard in April 1986.

The locomotive was completely stripped down allowing the frames to be grit blasted and painted. A new tender was built. Restoration continued and in 1997 *Eddystone* was re-wheeled with 1998 seeing the boiler craned back onto the frames. Further work continued on restoration with a first outing on the Swanage railway in 2003.

A giant of a locomotive, *Eddystone* weighs over 90 tons and has a top speed of 100 miles per hour. The diameters of the driving wheels are 6ft 2in and the length, complete with tender, is 65ft 5in.

Eddystone became a regular on the Somerset and Dorset route between Bournemouth and Bath between 1958 and 1962 and often photographed assisting the most famous of the S&D trains, The Pines Express overcoming the steep gradients of the Mendip Hills.

Opposite: Southern Locomotive Ltd's rebuilt West Country Class Bulleid Pacific No. 34028 Eddystone departs from Swanage.

The Swanage Railway offers a more thorough heritage steam and diesel timetable train service than virtually any other preserved railway, allowing visitors a unique journey through six miles of beautiful scenery. Passing the magnificent ruins of Corfe Castle, providing a valuable transport service for the local community, the line delightfully recreates the Southern Railway atmosphere.

The Swanage Railway Company (SRT) is responsible for the day to day operation of the Swanage Railway. All volunteers working on the railway are expected to comply with the company's policies and procedures in the same way as the company's employees.

The company is controlled by its Board of Directors with the General Manager responsible for the day to day management. The Board is responsible for appointing Directors. However, since the Swanage Railway Trust holds all the voting shares in the company, at least half of the Directors are always drawn from the Swanage Railway Trust's Council of Management.

The role of the Swanage Railway Trust is to set the agenda for the project through the Trust's policies and to perform a 'watching brief' over the day to day operations of the company. Inevitably raising both funds and the profile of the Swanage Railway project, form a major part of the Trust's activities.

Recollecting the halcyon days of steam with West Country Class 34028 Eddystone on a glorious summers day.

The Pinnacles and the chalk cliffs of Ballard Down are reflected in the azure sea on a tranquil day.

STUDLAND

Ballard Down to the north of Swanage is a chalk down once connected to the Needles on the Isle of Wight. The village of Studland is famed for its beaches, protected from the prevailing westerly winds by Old Harry; a natural assembly of sea stacks, natural arches and rocky promontories. The golden sands of Studland backed by the sand dunes of Studland Heath continue for over 2 miles where a narrow inlet allows Poole Harbour to drain into the sea, before the sand continues at Sandbanks.

The village of Studland lies under the shadow of Ballard Down with the church dating from Norman times and is dedicated to the patron Saint of sailors, St Nicholas. The church was rebuilt on the site of a Saxon church that would have been destroyed by Viking invaders in the ninth century. St Nicholas appears to have retained its original tower, unlike many churches where the towers were rebuilt during the prosperous 15th century.

The beach is backed by dunes that are in turn backed by the large area of Studland Heath. Little Sea is a fresh water lake, cut off from the sea as the dunes developed, and is now a rich habitat for birds and wintering wildfowl. The region has a plethora of footpaths that allow the entire area to be discovered taking in the western fringes of Poole Harbour. Both Studland and Godlingston Heath have been National Nature Reserves (NNR) since the mid 1940s. The site is also designated as an Area of Outstanding Natural Beauty and is a Site of Special Scientific Interest.

West of Studland is Godlingston Heath where a 400 tonne stone, Agglestone, can be found. Legend tells that the Devil threw it to its resting place from the Isle of Wight, although I suspect that it may well have something to do with erosion of the sand, leaving the stone standing proud. Other smaller examples can be seen including the Puckstone. Hidden among the pine forest are Britain's largest onshore oil fields and the BP Wytch Farm oil refinery. The Heathland and Studland Beach are owned and have been managed by the National Trust since 1982. The trust now maintains the scrub land and ensures the beach is kept tidy, as the area attracts over a million visitors a year.

The South West Coast Path National Trail makes use of Studland Beach ahead of reaching South Haven Point. A sculpture marks the end of the 630 mile coastal path that begins in Minehead on the edge of Exmoor in Somerset, or if walking in a clockwise direction, the start. Our journey has flirted with the long distance path since leaving Lyme Regis. Coastal paths came into being because the coastal fringes, once the haunt of smugglers, were also patrolled by the coastguard in pursuit of the contraband. In order for the coastguards to patrol the cliff tops, routes were created, enabling access to numerous tiny coves and sheltered bays. No longer used by coastguards the paths remain today as vantage points, to view the beautiful coastal scenery, away from the hustle and bustle of everyday life. The long distance path was completed in 1978 with the final section linking Somerset and Devon.

A sculpture marks the 630 mille South West Coast Path.

In 1940 the coastline of Studland was transformed, being one of two beaches in Dorset where the threat of invasion was seen as a major possibility, and was fortified as part of the anti-invasion preparations for World War Two.

By the summer of 1942 not only had the beach been commandeered but so to had the heathland between Studland and Poole Harbour, with the entire area closed to the public. The beach was used as mock landing zones in preparation for D-Day as it closely resembled the beach in France, where the invasion took place. The area would be graced by some of the most distinguished visitors including Winston Churchill, General Dwight D. Eisenhower, General Bernard Montgomery and Acting Admiral Louis Mountbatten who watched the trials from the observation post, nicknamed 'Fort Henry'. Built on top of Redland Point by Canadian troops, the fort took its name from a much earlier castle at Studland. During June 1944 prior to D-Day the area was said to be a hive of activity, with the bays crowded with shipping. Fort Henry, 90ft long with concrete walls 3ft deep remains one of Britain's most important relics of World War Two.

The variety of the Dorset landscape has ensured it has become a firm favourite with film and television programmes producers. Studland is no exception and followers of the 1970s TV series *Monty Python* may be familiar with the opening scene from the first episode, where Michael Palin staggers from the shallow sea, collapsing on the beach with Bournemouth in the background, saying, 'It's Monty Python's Flying Circus'.

This iconic cylindrical pillar box was first introduced in 1879 and is still in use today. The Royal Cipher dates installation during the reign of George VI. At one time the top would have had a post office direction sign attached.

Below and opposite: The church dates from Norman times and is dedicated to the patron saint of sailors, St Nicholas.

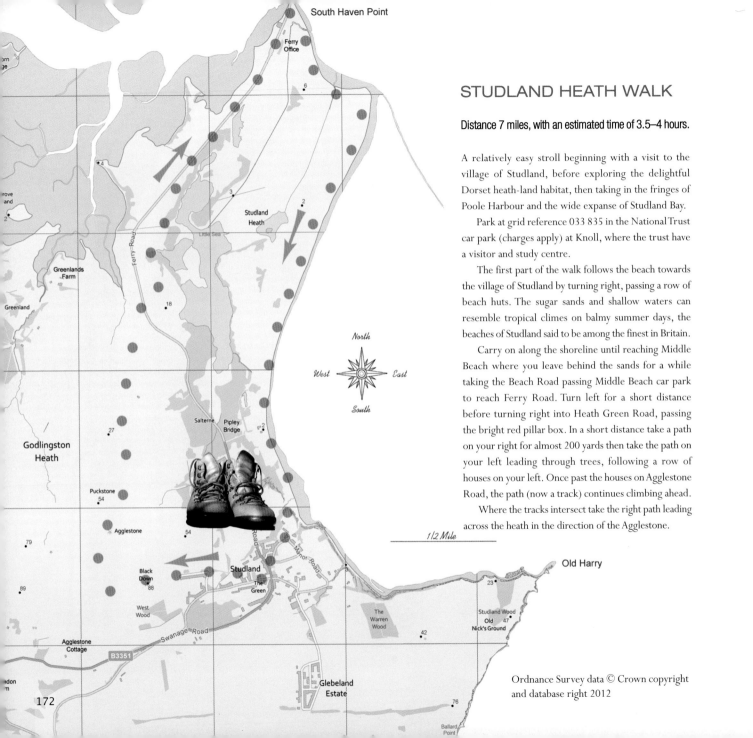

STUDLAND HEATH WALK

Distance 7 miles, with an estimated time of 3.5–4 hours.

A relatively easy stroll beginning with a visit to the village of Studland, before exploring the delightful Dorset heath-land habitat, then taking in the fringes of Poole Harbour and the wide expanse of Studland Bay.

Park at grid reference 033 835 in the National Trust car park (charges apply) at Knoll, where the trust have a visitor and study centre.

The first part of the walk follows the beach towards the village of Studland by turning right, passing a row of beach huts. The sugar sands and shallow waters can resemble tropical climes on balmy summer days, the beaches of Studland said to be among the finest in Britain.

Carry on along the shoreline until reaching Middle Beach where you leave behind the sands for a while taking the Beach Road passing Middle Beach car park to reach Ferry Road. Turn left for a short distance before turning right into Heath Green Road, passing the bright red pillar box. In a short distance take a path on your right for almost 200 yards then take the path on your left leading through trees, following a row of houses on your left. Once past the houses on Agglestone Road, the path (now a track) continues climbing ahead.

Where the tracks intersect take the right path leading across the heath in the direction of the Agglestone.

1/2 Mile

The striking white chalk of 'Old Harry' was formed during the cretaceous period over 65 million years ago.

Continue on the rough track for half a mile until you reach Agglestone on Black Down. A variation on the legend suggests that the Devil was trying to hit Corfe Castle, not Old Harry when he threw the stone from the Isle of Wight.

Studland Heath was the inspiration for Egdon Heath, which featured in Thomas Hardy's novel *The Return of the Native*. The heath is one of only a few sites in Britain that is home to all six native reptiles: these being the adder, grass snake, smooth snake, common lizard, sand lizard, and slow-worm. From the stone the route continues for over a mile across the heathland passing the Puckstone which, in years to come, may be another standing rock similar to the Agglestone. Ignoring tracks bearing left and right all the while heading in a northerly direction to reach a junction with Ferry Road.

The 400 tonne
Aggleston Rock.

The beaches of Shell Bay and Studland are of the most excellent quality golden sand.

Wytch Farm lies almost 3 miles north east from this junction; its oil wells dotted around the fringes of Poole Harbour are shielded by the conifer plantations, lessening their impact on the environment. The oil wells lie within the Jurassic Coast World Heritage Site and several areas fall within sites of Special Scientific Interest and Areas of Outstanding Natural Beauty, ensuring the well sites and main gathering site remain small and well screened.

Wytch Farm is one of the largest inland oilfields in Europe and began production in 1979. The Wytch Farm oil field consists of three unconnected oil reservoirs that lie under Poole Harbour and Poole Bay. The oil field produces vast quantities of oil and gas with the oil piped to a terminal at Hamble, on Southampton Water. From a peak of over 100,000 barrels of oil a day, production is now estimated to have fallen nearer to 15,000 barrels per day.

Once Ferry Road is attained turn left following the road for a mile and a half before reaching South Haven Point, and the ferry terminal. The route now following the road has its compensations with views opening out north-west across Poole Harbour to Brownsea Island and north-east to Sandbanks and Bournemouth.

An alternative lower route is to be found by taking a path on the right a short distance after joining the road, taking you through ferny scrub, with woods to your right. Hidden behind those woods lies Little Sea, a fresh-water lake cut off from the sea, its formation dating back several hundred years ago, created by the encroaching sand dunes, land locking a body of sea water.

The waters of the 'sea' are now fresh, draining from the heathland, eventually flowing to the sea. This area of dune land is the largest in southern Britain with the process of dune building still active today. For the next half a mile a number of paths lead off to the right taking you to the edge of the lake, where some hides have been built for observing the wildlife. This path is a lower route than the one that follows the road with the views to Poole Harbour at times hidden beyond the ridge.

An icon of the seaside, beach huts have a quintessential British feel, a place to shelter from a passing storm, and a place to brew a cup of tea. Some today are high specification and regimentally painted in vivid colours while others, as here at Studland, retain a more rustic charm.

After a mile rejoin the path following the road to reach South Haven Point and Shell Bay.

The ferry that connects Shell Bay to Sandbanks came into operation as a result of an Act of Parliament in 1923, granting the Bournemouth-Swanage Motor Road and Ferry Company to operate the service. The present ferry is 242ft in length and can accommodate up to 48 cars. The alternative route by road would result in a journey of some 25 miles to reach Sandbanks on the other side. The ferry runs daily, weather permitting, with the crossing time taking around four minutes.

The sculpture at South Haven Point observing the start or end of the 630 mile coastal path depicts many features to be seen along the national trail.

The return to the start point now follows the powdery sands of Studland Bay. During the summer months the vast expanse of beach can attract thousands of visitors daily with the most northerly stretch designated as a naturist area, said to be the UK's most popular naturist beach. The beach now has the official approval of the land owner, the National Trust who patrol the area and have well signposted the site. As Studland approaches and given the right weather conditions you could be forgiven for thinking you are in the Mediterranean, after all the beach was used for location shooting for the TV series *Only Fools and Horses* where it doubled as a beach in Benidorm. The car park is found by heading up past the National Trust visitor centre on Knoll Beach.

Ferry Road now leading back to Shell Bay, necessitates a crossing on the ferry to reach Sandbanks and Poole Harbour, ahead of our final destination, the bustling resort of Bournemouth. We are now leaving behind the idyll of the rural Dorset countryside, a magnificent seaboard that has been a constant companion for over 70 miles, only briefly punctuated by the charming seaside towns of Weymouth and Swanage.

Opposite: The South West Coast Path National Trail makes use of Studland Beach.

MINEHEAD 630mls

COAST PATH

THE BOURNEMOUTH-SWANAGE MOTOR ROAD AND FERRY COMPANY

The Bournemouth-Swanage Motor Road and Ferry Company came into being in July 1923 when an Act of Parliament received the Royal Assent, becoming law and giving the necessary powers for this statutory company to be created.

The idea of operating a car ferry service was largely the brainchild of Mr Frank Aman who came from Totland Bay on the Isle of Wight. His two sons, Gerard, an engineer, and Arthur, a stockbroker, assisted him. They were instrumental in starting the company and were also the largest individual shareholders who maintained their family connection until 1961.

The venture commenced with the building of two slipways and the new road from Studland, with an order placed for Ferry No. 1 with J. Samuel White, a well-known firm of shipbuilders on the Isle of Wight.

Stone for the slipways and the road foundations came from quarries on the Isle of Purbeck, mostly from the cliff-face quarry at Seacombe Cliffs. Barges carried the stone round by sea for the slipway foundations while primitive, one-speed lorries and Sentinel steam-driven wagons via Worth Matravers, Langton Matravers and Swanage brought stone for the road.

It was almost three years after the Act of Parliament was passed before Ferry No. 1 came into operation in July 1926. Ferry No. 1 was steam-driven and originally constructed to carry 15 cars; but after only a few years in service it was modified to enable 18 cars to be carried at any one time. The service was popular from the start and in the first rather short summer season 100,000 passengers and 12,000 cars were ferried across the 400yd entrance to Poole Harbour.

With the outbreak of World War Two the service became restricted. Events across the channel in 1943 saw the service closed to the public, and taken over by the military, in preparation for the D-Day landings.

At the end of the war the ferry was in need of an extensive refit and the road too required substantial repairs to bomb and shell craters. In addition the removal of tank traps and 'Dragons Teeth' obstacles would prevent the service being fully restored until 1946. Ferry No. 1 carried on gallantly for another 12 years but the repair periods became longer and the service was bedevilled by breakdowns.

The service runs daily with the crossing taking around four minutes.

The present ferry, *Bramble Bush Bay*, came into service in January 1994. The ferry is 242ft in length and can carry 48 cars.

DO NOT EMBARK
PROWS BEING RAISED

For a short while a second ferry was used, Ferry No. 2, also steam-driven having been purchased from its previous owners after it became redundant on the East to West Cowes service, on the Isle of Wight. The ferry only had space for eight cars and was really too small for use even in those days.

By the mid-1950s it was decided to replace the original steam ferry. The alternative replacements considered were a new ferry or a bridge, whichever met with most favour and support from local people. Many were against the idea of a bridge, which would, of necessity, have had to be at a high level and consequently would have dominated the view from all around the area. It was clear that any proposal to build a bridge would not gain sufficient support from the various local authorities, so a new ferry was ordered.

Ferry No. 3 was diesel-electric powered and carried a maximum of 28 cars. It had an overall length of 157ft, with a beam of 42ft 6in. It was equipped with three Ruston diesel engines and normally operated on two of these, although it could run on only one engine when necessary. This was a useful feature and meant that at least one engine acted as a spare at all times. Also repairs and strip-downs could be carried out without making any changes to the scheduled service times.

During the 35 years that it was in service Ferry No. 3 proved to be very reliable. Annually the ferry carried something in the order of 650,000 vehicles and, if vehicle passengers are included, well over 1 million people. Ferry No. 3 helped enormously to popularise the service, which over the years, attracted many regular users while providing a unique experience for visitors to the area, many of whom were prepared to wait in quite long queues in order to travel on the ferry.

Recent years have seen both slipways rebuilt with a new roundabout, and new toll booths constructed here, at Shell Bay.

The present ferry *Bramble Bush Bay* came into service in January 1994, the fourth to operate this service but the first to be named. It has been named after a small bay, located close to the Shell Bay side of the crossing, a bay where several houseboats have been stationed for at least the last 50 years.

Opposite and right: The ferry operates between a narrow channel using the chain to pull itself along. The chains, anchored on both banks, rest on the sea bed. Each chain is 1,235ft long and lasts 15 to 18 months. The chain is only powered on one side at a time, and is powered on the side away from the flow of the tide. The ferry uses its motors to pull itself along progressively raising the chain from the bottom and lowering it again behind the direction of travel.

POOLE HARBOUR

Poole Harbour was formed at the end of the last ice age, now home to the estuary of several rivers. The largest of these being the River Frome with its source in Evershot, a small hamlet some 550ft above sea level on the Dorset Downs. Its journey to the sea covering some 30 miles, takes a course north of the historic town of Dorchester before reaching Wareham and its confluence with the River Piddle, ahead of flowing quietly into Poole Harbour. Despite the surface of Poole Harbour covering some 14sq miles, the average depth is a mere 18in. A channel is regularly dredged through the harbour to give access to the many passenger, cargo and pleasure boats that use the harbour. It has been said that Poole is the second largest natural harbour in the world, although this fact is disputed by several worldwide, including Cork in Ireland, New Zealand's Kaipara Harbour and San Francisco Bay, California.

The notable features of the harbour, as well as its beautiful setting, are the numerous islands, the largest being Brownsea Island which is managed by the National Trust, with a good deal of the island open to the public, including areas of woodland and heath all enjoying a broad variety of wildlife.

The Waterfront Museum Poole houses a rich history of the ancient port, revealed on four floors of galleries housed in a 19th-century quayside warehouse. Exhibits in the museum include the famous Poole Log Boat, numerous pictures and maps of the area and items recovered from the Studland Bay wreck.

BROWNSEA ISLAND

Brownsea Island is now one of the few places in England where red squirrels survive, due to the non native grey squirrel not being introduced to the island. The red squirrel also thrives on the island helped no doubt by the large crop of cones from the Scots Pine that cover the island. The island is designated a habitat of national and international importance for a variety of birds including dunlin, kingfishers, common and sandwich terns and oystercatchers. The island has been described by Bill Oddie as 'the best place for seeing wildlife in Dorset'.

The north part of Brownsea Island is leased to the Dorset Wildlife Trust and access is restricted, only gained by the accompaniment of a guide who conducts tours during July and August. The area includes a large lagoon which supports migrating birds and wildfowl.

The first record of human activity dates back to the ninth century when a small chapel dedicated to St Andrew was built by the monks from Cerne Abbey.

In 1907 Robert Baden-Powell, a former British soldier, ran an experimental camp on Brownsea Island to try out his ideas about youth training, drawing on his experience in the army. He brought together 20 boys, some from public schools and some from working-class homes, and put them into camp under his leadership. His book *Scouting for Boys* was published in 1908, in six fortnightly parts. Sales of the books were remarkable and boys soon formed themselves into Scout Patrols. What had been intended as a training aid for existing organisations became the handbook of a new and, ultimately, worldwide movement.

Girls wanted to become part of the movement, with Baden-Powell and his sister Agnes Baden-Powell introducing Girl Guides in 1910, a parallel movement for girls, sometimes named Girl Scouts.

The island came under the control of the National Trust in 1962 who set aside almost 50 acres for Scout and Guide camping, an area that can accommodate up to 400. No other camping is allowed on the island.

Brownsea Island is only open mid March to early November with an admission fee payable. A ferry can be taken from Sandbanks next to the Studland ferry terminal.

Less than a quarter of a mile off the western shore of Brownsea Island lays Furzey Island. The island has a hidden secret for it is home to one of the oil wells and gathering stations for Wytch Farm.

The island was fortified in 1547 against invasion from Europe by means of a blockhouse, which became known as Brownsea Castle, also known as Branksea Castle.

The coastline from Sandbanks to Christchurch is eroding and a programme of beach re-nourishment and the construction of 'rock groynes' was established to prevent the beach from being washed away. The rock groynes not only provide a fascinating feature but have proved positive ecologically with the increase in lichens followed by barnacles and seaweed, limpets, anemones and crab.

SANDBANKS AND POOLE

Now close to the main resort of Bournemouth, the B3369 circumnavigates Sandbanks, perhaps one of the most affluent parts of the UK. The small peninsula is home to some of the most expensive properties in Britain, now as famous for its well known residents as it is for its glorious golden sands. Often thought of as one of the best beaches on the south coast, its fine sands gently shelve to the often azure sea.

North of Sandbanks is Poole, with Bournemouth adjoining to the east. The first inhabitants of Poole can be traced back to before the Iron Age. Durotriges, one of the Celtic tribes living in Britain before the Roman invasion, moved from the hilltop settlements at Maiden Castle and colonised the heathland around the harbour. The Romans landed here during their conquest of Britain. During the Norman invasion in the 11th century the port was growing but Poole is not mentioned in the *Domesday Book*. Records show that the name Poole first came into being during the 12th century, a time when the town was developing as a principal port, with the increasing trade in wool a major influence. During the 18th century the port was said to have been one of the busiest in Britain. Today Poole facilitates a commercial port with cross channel ferries operating out of the harbour, the maritime theme continuing with the town being the headquarters of the RNLI.

An attractive assortment of shells can be found on the shoreline at sandbanks.

BOURNEMOUTH

In the early part of the 19th century the area was still barren heathland. The mouth of the Bourne River was uninhabited, perhaps only visited by a few fishermen and the haunt of smugglers in the 16th century. The heathland became part of a hunting estate but by the late 1700s had become neglected, only occupied by a cottage close to the stream. In 1809 the first public house The Tapps Arms was built on the heath. In 1801 Lewis Tregonwell, a retired army officer began building villas for tourists. By the 1830s a small community had built up with a scattering of houses, villas and cottages.

The physician and writer Augustus Granville, author of *The Spas of England*, visited in 1841. The book described health resorts around the country and he included a chapter on Bournemouth in the second edition of his book. The publication of the book, as well as the growth of visitors to the seaside seeking the medicinal use of the seawater and the fresh air of the pines, helped the town to grow and establish itself as an early tourist destination. By 1851 the population had increased to almost 700 with that figure more than doubling a decade later. The pleasure gardens were laid out in the 1870s and by the turn of the century the population had again increased to almost 60,000. The town by this time had taken in the growing nearby villages to the east of Boscombe, Westbourne and Southbourne. The town grew further by the 1930s with its boundary extended north and east.

It was the arrival of the railway that would eventually help to accelerate the popularity and the development of the town. The railways first arrived in 1840; the route from Brockenhurst to Wareham was diverted across the heathland to avoid the New Forest, the line becoming known locally as Castleman's Corkscrew, named after the Wimborne solicitor who promoted the line. With the town still a mere handful of houses, it was deemed far too insignificant to have a station, the nearest being opened in Poole on a short branch from the mainline.

By the mid 1800s much opposition was heard about the railway coming to Bournemouth fearing it would open up the exclusive health resort to day trippers, 1862 did, however, see the coming of the railways closer to Bournemouth with a station opening at Christchurch. It would be another eight years before finally coming to Bournemouth with a single platform station opening, known as Bournemouth East.

Bournemouth can boast not one but three cliff railways along its curving arc of seven miles of golden sands. The second cliff railway was opened here at West Cliff in August 1908.

An idyllic scene on the golden sands of Bournemouth.

1874 saw a second station opening, Bournemouth West, an extension on the line from Poole, served by the Somerset & Dorset Joint Railway, often referred to as the S&D connecting Bath to Bournemouth, with a continuation of a through route to the Midlands. The line, as we have already heard, was affectionately known as the 'Slow & Dirty' in the main due to the line having to carry freight and local passenger traffic up over the Mendip Hills in Somerset. The summer did, however, bring increased volumes of traffic to the line, with the through route, from the Midlands, bringing fully packed Saturday summers services to Bournemouth. The S&D always had an affectionate following from railway enthusiasts, and when the Beeching axe fell in 1966 it was widely mourned.

The original Bournemouth East situated on Holdenhurst Road was replaced by a new station in 1885 on the opposite side of the road, a far grandiose affair more in keeping of the growing town and reflecting the Winter Gardens. The station became known as Bournemouth Central in 1899 until 1967 when it took its present title, Bournemouth Railway Station.

The new pier was opened in 1880. Extensions have since been added and major repair work carried out to the structure with the overall length now in excess of 1,000ft.

The first pier in Bournemouth was built in 1856, no more than just a short wooden jetty and was soon replaced with a longer structure in 1861. The wooden piles were replaced by cast iron in 1866 but these proved short lived with the pier suffering storm damage in 1867, the landing stage being swept away. Repairs carried out prolonged the pier's life for a further decade before another severe gale rendered the structure unsafe.

A new pier was designed at a cost of over £20,000 and opened in 1880. Extensions have since been added and major repair work carried out to the structure with the overall length now in excess of 1,000ft. During the 1970s a major programme of restoration took place costing some £1.7 million.

Bournemouth can boast not one, but three cliff railways along its curving arc of seven miles of golden sands. The first to be opened was the East Cliff Railway in April 1908. The line extends to 170ft and has two passenger cars running on parallel tracks. The winding gear is electrically operated, housed in the upper station and controlled by the driver. The early 'cars' were of wooden construction but were replaced by aluminium versions during the 1960s.

The second cliff railway opened a few months later on West Cliff, a little shorter in length, at 145ft.

The third, Fisherman's Walk Railway, opened in 1935, built close to Southbourne and Boscombe some 2 miles east of the East Cliff Railway. The railways normally operate between April and October.

The rock groynes continue eastward from Sandbanks to the pier at Bournemouth.

Created by the Victorians, the Bournemouth Pleasure Gardens cover 45 acres and run down to the seafront.

Bournemouth Pleasure Gardens are set out in the heart of the town and lie straddling the shallow waters of the Bourne River, from which the town takes its name. Created in the 19th century, the gardens cover 45 acres and run down to the seafront at the mouth of the river, beside the pier. One modern day attraction to the gardens is the Bournemouth Eye, an enormous helium filled balloon that acts as an observation point 500ft above the town, providing passengers with a spectacular bird's-eye view of the town and coastline.

Beach huts are now a quintessential character of the seaside and dominate the seafront here at Bournemouth, and as we have seen, their basic design can take many forms.

The town has a number of excellent museums and art galleries and bus tours are available. We should, however, not leave Bournemouth without mentioning the beach, and what a beach.

Nestled beneath a magnificent cliff line, the bay enjoys its own micro-climate, some of the warmest sea temperatures in the UK and stunning views of the Isle of Wight and the Isle of Purbeck. Whatever you want from a day at the beach, you'll find it all here. Whether it's relaxing in a deck chair, or simply strolling along the traditional seaside promenade. Traditional deck chairs can be hired all along the beach: simply help yourself and an attendant will collect the hire charge once you're settled.

It is now time to reflect on the journey that has covered over 80 miles of glorious coastline, perhaps some of the most diverse in Britain. A journey that began at Lyme Regis with its iconic Cobb, rich in history, our first introduction to the Dorset coast. The small town at the western extreme of Dorset, had by the late 18th century, become a popular seaside resort among the middle classes, but would become known throughout the country for its famous fossil finds. The small settlements, once the haunt of smugglers, of Seatown, Eype and Burton Bradstock are complemented by the larger town of Bridport with its harbour located at West Bay. For the next 16 miles the bulk of Chesil Beach dominated the seaboard.

At the eastern extreme of Chesil Beach, on the Isle of Portland, a large limestone outcrop creates the most southerly point of Dorset, Portland Bill. The larger seaside towns of Weymouth and Swanage bring many visitors to the area and between these two delightful seaside towns the chalk cliffs again, once the haunt of smugglers, were discovered, with the area providing a plethora of walking options among some of the most dramatic and picturesque coastline in England. Oil exploration has been going on for many decades but the areas outstanding natural beauty has been retained, as most of the activity is well shielded as we discovered near to Studland. The short ferry ride brought us to Sandbanks and Bournemouth, a bustling seaside town, in complete contrast to the solitude of the majority of the charming, picturesque Dorset coast. The journey of discovery has been a delight to take and I hope the book will encourage you to visit, as you can be assured of a warm welcome.

The traditional time to visit is during the summer, but equally impressive would be to come during winter when stormy days and tranquil mild days will provide you with inspiration. Perhaps my favourite to time to visit, but I will keep that to myself. Thank you for joining me on this wonderful journey of discovery.